Investing for Survival in the '80s

THE HOW TO BEAT INFLATION BOOK

By the Contributing Editors of
The MoneyLetter

Edited by Richard Starks

The Contributing Editors of
The MoneyLetter
include:

Dr. Morton Shulman

Avner Mandelman,
analyst with Bache Halsey Stuart Canada Ltd.

David Louis, LL.B., C.A.,
National Tax Manager of Ernst & Whinney,
Chartered Accountants

Gary Weiss,
a business writer and real-estate specialist

Roy Hardaker, M.B.A., F.C.S.I.

David Cowan, C.A.

Investing for Survival in the '80s

THE HOW TO BEAT INFLATION BOOK

Published by
Financial Education Services
A Division of Hume Publishing Limited
716 Gordon Baker Road, Willowdale, Ontario M2H 3M8

Distributed by
McGraw-Hill Ryerson
330 Progress Avenue, Scarborough, Ontario M1P 2Z5

Investing for Survival in the '80s

The How to Beat Inflation Book

Canadian Cataloguing in Publication Data

Main entry under title:
Investing for survival in the 80's

ISBN 0-919255-00-0

1. Investments-Canada. 2. Finance, Personal.
I. Starks, Richard. II. The MoneyLetter.
HG4521.158 332.6'78'0971 C80-094798-3

Printed and Durabound
in Canada by
Webcom Limited

Book design by Carl Brett

Contents

Introduction by Dr. Morton Shulman: how to prosper in the coming cataclysm

I think it is essential for an investor today to understand the political, social and economic changes taking place in this country. If you don't, you will always be making your investment decisions against an unknown or misunderstood background. And that, of course, can be fatal. It's for this reason that I've devoted my introduction to an overview of the 1980s.

As you know, Canada entered the new decade in deep economic trouble. Our $10-billion annual deficit was (and is) proportionately the highest in the Western world. The United States, with ten times the population and economic base, plus huge military expenditures, runs a $30-billion deficit. As for our other trading partners, such as Japan, Germany, Switzerland and the Soviet Union, they have no deficit at all. This makes us roughly comparable to the ne'er-do-well cousin who is living high off the hog, earning $15,000 a year but spending $25,000, and making up the difference with IOUs. Sooner or later, no one will take those IOUs.

Canada's IOUs are called dollars. And, as we pump out more and more of them, nations and individuals around the world will show increasing reluctance to accept them. So they will become worth less and less. This condition prevailed throughout the late 1970s and it is bound to accelerate in the early 1980s. And just as the external value of the dollar will fall, so will its value at home. So prices will rise. I can easily foresee an annual inflation rate of 25%-35% by 1985 — perhaps even higher, depending on our politicians.

Actually, our politicians have very little leeway of action. Theoretically they could slash government expenditures and drastically raise taxes so as to balance the budget and stop the inflation and the erosion of our dollar. But practically speaking, any such action, no matter how minor, would meet with tremendous resistance. The simple fact is that Canadians have grown to believe that today's high standard of living is their right, and any government that attempts to cut that standard will speedily be replaced by a more amenable one. Can any MP be elected from the Atlantic Provinces, if he suggests a cut in transfer of payments or a sizable reduction of unemployment insurance benefits? Can any MP be elected from Quebec, if he agrees to cut mothers' allowances? Can any MP be elected from Ontario, if he tries to raise income taxes? Can any MP be elected from the West if he agrees to stop the subsidization of freight rates or if he agrees to the imposition of large taxes on the oil companies? Not bloody likely. And there will always be an opposition who will say, "Elect us, and we will reverse these harsh policies."

No, the politicians will find it easier to go along, to temporize, to decry inflation publicly, but to keep the printing presses rolling in the background, turning out more and more dollars. What this means is that, by the mid 1980s, inflation of 30% will be accompanied by a prime rate of 20%, first mortgages of 25%, and a credit crunch. It is almost inevitable that interest rates will rise, because it makes no sense for anyone to lend money at a rate lower than the inflation rate, for the lender would then be losing money every day the loan was outstanding. The credit crunch will develop as more and more lenders stop lending in Canada, and either seek a foreign haven for their money, or else buy goods instead — land, buildings, gold, art or antiques.

This onset of high inflation and higher interest rates will put tremendous pressure on the government to do something, and that something inevitably will be price and wage controls as an initial move. The problem, though, in galloping inflation, is that price controls can't work, because we must import too many of our goods. This results in shortages and then in black markets, where scarce goods are obtainable at much higher prices than the controlled ones. The government then has the choice of removing the controls on the goods that are in short supply, or (more acceptable politically) imposing rationing. As the flow of capital out of Canada speeds up — it's already running at a rate of $1-billion per year — the government will probably impose restrictions on the outflow, possibly bringing in foreign exchange controls and banning non-essential purchases of foreign goods. Citizens will be forbidden to take money out of the country for foreign vacations (although those vacations will be so expensive that few people could afford them in any case).

The major turning point will probably occur during the second half of the decade, in the course of a federal election. By that time there will be general disillusionment with the old parties, and fringe candidates pushing various economic nostrums will spring up by the hundred. Much to their amazement, extremist parties, such as the Marxist-Leninists on the left and the Libertarians on the right, will actually elect a few candidates. And a party forthrightly expressing the disillusionment of the people — such as the Rhinoceros party — could well elect several dozen members.

In such an atmosphere, it is almost certain that the

main opposition party (Tories?), desperately searching for a popular election issue, will come forth with indexing — the Brazilian and Israeli "solution." Superficially, indexing is the perfect solution, for it takes the bite out of inflation. Basically, all that happens is that, on the first of every month, everything is revalued upward by that month's inflation rate — bank deposits, mortgages, pensions, salaries, and so on — so that the ordinary worker does not continue to see his standard of living continue to slide. In a galloping inflation, such a proposal is very seductive, and it would probably be instituted by the government in power before the election, "so as to keep out the irresponsible opposition."

The problem with indexing, though, is that it removes every restraint *against* inflation. There is no longer any incentive for the government to keep up the struggle, so the printing presses will really begin to roll, leading to a total collapse of the external value of the country's currency. Because of this, imports will only be purchasable with gold or by barter. Our gold reserves will soon be exhausted, while our bartering ability is dependent on grain and on wood. Actually, only the grain markets are secure, for there is a tremendous expansion of wood production taking place in South America, and we can't compete with it because of our slower growing climate. The pulp market may therefore be lost by the late 1980s. Also, we cannot set ever higher prices for wheat, because of the competition from Australia and the U.S., so there just won't be enough foreign exchange to finance all our imports.

This means that non-essential foreign goods such as oranges and television sets will become more and more expensive and difficult to find, and the standard of living will fall precipitously. This will be accompanied by a flight of the rich to more profitable and stable countries, while the size of the bureaucracy will increase five-fold to administer the many new regulations and to guard the borders and search the mail to ensure that no money or valuables is being sent or taken out of the country.

By the late 1980s, the flight from paper money will be in its final stages. Gold will sell at $2,000 or $3,000 an ounce, and our gasoline, largely coming from the tar sands, will be rationed at $10 a gallon. Oddly enough, people will be able to buy less and less of everything, even though they will have more paper money in their pockets than ever before. Silver will disappear from circulation. Religion will flourish, and dozens of new cults will spring up as people search for something to have faith in.

How will it all end? The same way it has ended in every other country that has suffered inflation: with a cataclysmic political change as the people turn away from the politicians who have failed them and seek some national hero — perhaps on a white horse or perhaps from the extreme left or right — who will impose a harsh new regime with a reconstituted currency backed by gold (or oil?) and a balanced budget. And when will this happen? I predict the early 1990s.

The depressing end to this story is that there is no Canadian politician to whom I have spoken who does not agree that this is the road we are following. So we have about a decade to prepare for the bad times to come — a decade in which we must plan our investments to ward off the ravages of inflation and to build up our capital and other resources so that we can not just survive, but prosper.

Dr. Morton Shulman

Part 1

THE STOCK MARKET

First, Know Yourself: gamblers, speculators and investors

Most people accept that the stock market is still one of the best ways to get ahead of inflation and make your money grow. It's true that in recent years the performance of the Toronto Stock Exchange 300 Index or the Dow Jones Industrial Average has not been particularly impressive, and at times has shown a real decline in value. But few people invest in the total market. Most invest in specific individual stocks. And there have certainly been many individual stocks that have risen in value at a rate far above the rate of increase in the overall market and far above the rate of increase in the cost of living. The trick, of course, is to choose the right stocks. That requires an understanding of the way the stock market works. And that is what this section of the book is all about.

Before you make your first investment, however, you have to decide what kind of approach you are going to take toward the market. What kind of approach, in fact, is best for you. As a starting point, you have probably heard a friend tell you about the great score he made in the market — about how he bought Wishful Thinking Oil and Gas at 15 cents a share and now it's worth $4.50. Drilling results have been fantastic and a major oil company is planning to buy the stock at $12.50 per share. If you are like everyone else, you probably think: "How did he do it? I never seem to get a chance like that." This is a classic example of gambling in the stock market. And as in all gambling situations, be it at the dice tables or at the races, you only hear about the winners.

As a real example, Cuvier Mines Ltd. in 1972-73 held a lead-zinc prospect in Nova Scotia. Cuvier managed to link up with Imperial Oil Ltd.'s mining arm, Imperial Oil Developments, to do some diamond drilling on the claims. As a result of this, and of substantial promotion, the shares moved in a short period of time from approximately 60 cents to a high of $5.25. Results, however, were not sufficiently attractive to bring the property into production as a mine. And in 1974 the shares plunged back to 61 cents, the level they're still close to today.

In this instance, the gambler bought Cuvier stock on the expectation that the drilling result would be favorable. He hoped that this would be one company, out of many hundreds over the years, that would produce an ore-body, finance a mine, show earnings and eventually be worth many dollars. This is typical of the gambler. He plays the long odds with the hope (and probably prayer) for huge and rapid gains. He trades on gossip, hot tips, promotions and usually small amounts of money in penny stocks. These "penny dreadfuls" allow him to buy a substantial number of shares for a few hundred dollars. Generally, if not successful, he is prepared to lose these dollars. The gambler is, as a rule, ignorant of what he is doing, and why he's doing it. He has limited experience in the stock market and is often the victim of high-pressure selling tactics and greed. Nevertheless, the gambler is a common sight in the stock market.

When you put money into the market, you have to decide on your approach. Are you going to be a gambler or are you going to try to adopt an approach that is more sophisticated and intelligent? Essentially, there are only three approaches that you can choose from. Gambling is one; the other two are speculating and investing. The one that you select will depend on a number of factors —

your objectives, your knowledge of the market, the amount of money you have available, your personality, and so on. It is important, though, that you make a conscious decision on which approach you are going to adopt. This will help you determine where you, personally, fit into the market. And it will also help you decide which market opportunities you are going to take advantage of. It will, in other words, help reduce the over-choice of opportunities to more manageable proportions.

As we say, the gambler tends to have limited market experience and has little idea of what he is doing. Probably, he shouldn't be in the market at all. But what about the speculator and the investor? In what way are they different?

Basically, a speculator takes risks, but unlike the gambler, he only takes risks that are calculated. He always knows what he is doing, and he always has a good reason for doing it. His approach is essentially fundamental. He analyzes and weighs; he tries to determine how long it will be before "the street" will also like the stocks he speculates in. His aim is the greatest possible return measured against the risks involved. Losses will be cut quickly and decisively at predetermined levels. If a stock does not perform to his expectations in his time-frame, then he gets out. He is not greedy. He knows that there has to be a generally recognizable profit potential remaining in a stock when he sells it, or he will not be able to achieve his objectives.

The speculator knows what he is doing because he understands and appraises the stock. He is knowledgeable, aggressive, experienced, sophisticated and satisfied with a return within his parameters. His tools include technical analysis as well as fundamental analysis, and he makes great use of such techniques as option writing and buying, rights, warrants, margin debt, and convertible debentures for leverage. (We'll have more to say about these later.) His prime aim is good timing. He wants to be first in and second-last out. The speculator makes up his own mind, and, although he may take his broker's recommendations, he often selects his speculations himself.

An illustration of the stance and play a speculator might have made is Dome Petroleum in January, 1977. The stock had been cyclical and volatile, but it seemed to have great potential for the long term. At that time, it was trading in the $54-$56 range. The speculator would have believed that with the drilling season approaching in the Beaufort Sea, plus a number of other factors, a price move was imminent. To participate in this move, but to control his risk, the speculator might have purchased a call option that could be exercised at $65 per share, expiring in the third week of October, 1977. The call option would have cost him $8 per share. For one contract to buy 100 shares at $65, the speculator would have paid about $828, including brokerage. His maximum loss would have been that $828. As for his profit, that would have been enormous. In October, 1977, Dome shares reached $106. His option then had an intrinsic value of $41 per share.

Now we come to the supposed "fuddy-duddy" approach of the group — investing. The investor is portrayed as methodical, conservative, long-range and fundamental in his view of stocks. He is. However, his objectives are different from those of the speculator. His concerns are with more mundane considerations such as safety and conservation of capital, protection against inflation, return, tax aspects of dividends and interest income, portfolio building, diversification by security, industry, risk and geography — all of which are, of course, quite valid concerns. He looks carefully at what he buys and sells, weighs recommendations and makes his own decisions. Nevertheless, he can come through with some astounding results in his stock purchases.

For example, suppose that in the spring of 1976, after analysis of his portfolio and the market in general, the investor believed that the Bank of Montreal, with its higher yield and lower price-earnings ratio than the other chartered banks, was still safe and secure for his account. Also, he believed that the new management might in two to three years' time change the market's assessment of the stock.

In the spring of 1976, he could have purchased 100 Bank of Montreal shares for approximately $1,535, including brokerage. The bank paid a dividend of 98 cents per share to yield 6.4% and had earned $2.37 for a price-earnings ratio of 6.5. In June, 1976, he would have been able to purchase an additional 11 shares at $14 for a cost of $154. A further rights issue in September, 1977 would have allowed him to purchase 13 shares at $14.25 each for a cost of $185.25. A third rights issue in August, 1978 gave the investor the opportunity for the purchase of 17 shares at $20 each for a cost of $340.

Thus, in February, 1978 he would have owned 141 shares for a total investment of $2,214.25 or $15.70 per share. His dividend would then have been $1.24 per share, for a return of 7.9% on his original investment. The market price was $26.50. He would have made an unrealized capital gain of $10.80 per share, or $1,523, and increased his return from 6.4% to 7.9%. At the time, that wasn't bad for the long-term conservative fundamentalist — although today, the steady investor might reasonably expect to do better than this.

The point is, though, that it is possible to make money by adopting any one of the three approaches. In each case, though, the characteristics are very different, both in terms of the objectives and in the way that those objectives are reached. You should decide which one best suits you, and then you should tailor your stock market moves to make sure that you are following the best approach. The results you achieve will then be consistent with your objectives, and you will always be sure that you are operating in the area of the market that is right for you.

Measuring Risk: how to tell if the dog's going to bite you

As you probably know, one of the reliable maxims of the stock market is that the higher the risk you take, the greater the potential return you stand to earn. Clearly, as an astute investor, you want to maximize that potential return. But at the same time, you can see that there must come a point where you say to yourself, the added potential return just isn't worth the added risk.

As you can imagine, this point varies widely from one individual to another, and only you can decide where this point occurs for you personally. Do you enjoy risk? Thrive on it? Hate it? Fear it? Or merely take the approach that everything in life involves some kind of risk so why waste time worrying about it? This, of course, ties in with your decision on whether you are a gambler, a speculator or an investor. But whatever your answer to these questions on risk, it will probably be incomplete — until you can find some method of measuring risk in a quantifying way. Just exactly how much risk *is* involved in a given investment? Since this is a fundamental question that you will probaly be asking yourself each time you consider an investment decision, let's examine it in some detail.

The "risk-quantifying" methods we discuss here are all based on the following assumption: Once you thoroughly research an investment, you will possess far more information than you realize. This information sometimes shows itself in "gut feelings," which are difficult to accept as a basis for rational decision-making. Yet this information is valuable. We will therefore describe several ways that may help you to extract such information from your own "memory-banks." The methods are all based on the research of David Hertz of the Stanford Research Institute in California, and they are widely used in industry.

Let's assume you have done some diligent research on International Risks Ltd. — now trading at $20 per share — and that you contemplate investing in its shares. You have read the financial statements of the company, the press releases, the newspaper clippings, and all the material you could find on its product line. You are now a reasonably informed investor, and have an intuitive "feel" for the company's prospects. How do you now translate that feel into hard information?

Let us pose a series of questions, which you can answer to the best of your subjective knowledge. The answers may not be precise, but if your research was good, the chances are your answers will be close to the real prospects of the company. These prospects will be reflected in the "risk profile" table we will now create for the stock. Let us ask: What are the chances that the stock (now at $20) will rise within a year to more than $22? We will assume you have answered (after some soul searching) that the chances are about 50%. Now, what are the chances that the stock will rise above $24 within a year? You say 20%. And above $26? Say 10%. And $28? You say 0%. We will now do the same for the downside risk. What are the chances, in your estimation, that the stock will remain above $20? Say you decide it is about 60%.

And above $18? Let's assume you say it is 80%. And above $16? Say you come up with 100%.

The results are summarized in the following table:

Your estimate of the lowest price of the stock after one year of holding it	*Per cent chance for occurrence of event*
$16	100%
$18	80%
$20 (present price)	60%
$22	50%
$24	20%
$26	10%
$28	0%

Some of the elementary meanings of the list: Your chances of gaining are 60%; or, to express that differently, you have three chances out of five of selling the stock for more than you bought it for. Also, there is no chance that the stock will trade above $28, or below $16 (according to your estimates). Note that the figure of, say, 80% beside the $18 means two equivalent things: Either the chances of the stock trading above $18 are 80%; or the chances of the stock trading below $18 are 20%.

Let us now devise some uses for this "information" we now have about the stock, dealing in absolute dollars. Suppose you intend to invest $1,000 in the stock. You now choose an arbitrary point of 20% failure (you may choose another at your convenience), and see that, at this chance of gain of four out of five, you may turn an investment of $20 per share into either $24 or $18. This is according to your own gut feeling, clothed with numbers. Now, assuming you purchase 100 shares with your $1,000 (at a margin of 50%), you could either gain $400 or lose $200. Would you enter into such a game? Would you risk $200 to gain $400? Only you can decide if this degree of risk is acceptable to you personally, but at least you have a concrete question on which to base your decision.

Another way of using the information in the table is to decide in advance on a required rate of return. Say you are greedy and want a return of 40% on your investment. On your $1,000 you would require a gain of $400. You would look at the table and see that you have a four out of five chance of making this profit. We will assume that you decide that this chance is acceptable to you. But what about the risk? From the table, you can see that you would risk losing up to $200. (Basically, this is the same example as the one we used above, except we start by considering the potential, or desired, gain, rather than the potential, or acceptable, loss.) Again, only you can decide if the potential gains outweigh the potential losses.

You can see, then, that the table you have constructed will not provide you with the "final" answer to the investment question. But it will help you put your own research into use. In other words, forcing yourself to quantify your gut-feeling for the stock's prospects will not guarantee you a surefire method of correctly guessing whether the stock will go up. However, if you have researched the stock properly, it will enable you to use more of your knowledge than you would otherwise have done. This decision-making-in-risky-circumstances is widely used by several large corporations. It does not ensure that any particular project will be successful, but rather that in the long run the total portfolio of investments will be successful. In the same way, you could not say with certainty that any particular acquisition of stock will be successful. But in the long run, over several purchases of stock, your ability to make money will improve since you will be basing your investment decisions on more information.

It is common for corporate planning specialists to provide "likely" and "unlikely" scenarios, with various levels of probability. Econometric forecasters also provide their clients with more than one forecast of the economy, and assign different probabilities to the occurrences (see any forecast of Chase Econometrics, or D.R.I. of Canada, for instance). The common characteristic in all these techniques, however, is that they use the gut feeling acquired in research, and then quantify it subjectively.

One way of using the table you have constructed is a refinement (called a convergence toward a fixed value, if you want to be technical). The concept is simple. When do you stop studying the facts you have gathered about a company and go to look for new information? When have you extracted the full value of the information you have in your hands? You can probably guess the answer. All through your research of the stock, you query yourself and modify your estimates for that stock. For example, you discover that the prospects of a new product are rosier than you had previously imagined. Therefore, you upgrade the prospects for the company's stock. The moment your refinement (still based on nothing else but your own gut feeling) does not lead to appreciable change in the table of probabilities, you have probably reached the point where the information in your hands is fully digested. If you still feel you need to study the company some more, by all means do so, but you would be well advised to look for new information to supplement the information already in your hands.

Suppose now that you have thoroughly studied the company and constructed your "final" risk table. And suppose that it shows you that the risk involved in investing in that company is greater than you would like to accept. What should you do? (The decision is easy if your risk table shows that the risk is worth taking: You go ahead and invest.) Most likely, you would go back to your final risk table and have one more look at it — to see if you could upgrade your estimates to make the risk worthwhile. If you can do this — legitimately, and with a clear conscience — then you may invest.

If you cannot bring yourself to change your opinion of the stock's prospects, and you still feel like investing in the stock, then you may have to admit that you are going to accept a risk not commensurate with the reward. If you then go ahead and invest, that's acceptable — as long as you know what you are doing, and appreciate you are taking more risk than you would normally like. If you decide not to invest because in your terms the potential reward does not justify the risk, then you may later find you have avoided a costly investment error.

Basic Research: know who you're going to get into bed with

If you are like many investors, the chances are that when you buy something like a television set you will do a lot more research than you will when you buy securities. First of all, you will probably shop around. You'll inquire about the manufacturer's reputation, ask friends who have the same model if they are satisfied, visit different stores and compare prices. Yet, when you buy shares, you may not even look at the annual report of the company you are investing in. This makes no sense — because, unless you are buying 100 shares of a stock trading at less than $5, you will be spending more on your stocks than on your television set. Shouldn't you know more about the company? After all, you are paying hundreds, or even thousands, of dollars for a share in it.

So let's have a look at the basic research steps you should take before buying a security. For purposes of clarity, we will dwell on two types of securities: common stocks, and commodity futures contracts. (The discussion on common stocks would also apply to bonds issued by a company.) A common stock, as you know, is a certificate of ownership of a business, and a business is an organization that produces a cash flow. In order for a stock to be worth anything to you, it has to produce an income for you, either in the form of dividends or a capital gain.

Before you buy into a stock, you should picture yourself as intending to buy the whole company, not just a piece of it. This will force you to assess it properly. Remember, you are depositing your money in the hands of strangers. Wouldn't you like to know first what they are up to? You should learn as much as you can about the company, its affairs, its management and its finances. Also learn about the areas of business that the company is in. This might mean a trip to your local business library to look up as much background material as you can. It would certainly involve a call to your broker, a lengthy conversation with an analyst who follows the company's fortunes on a regular basis, and an examination of the company's most recent financial statements. All this is standard practice. But is there not something else you should do?

Briefly — yes, there is. And it's something that most investors do not do. If it's at all possible, you should make an effort to see the physical buildings, plant, offices, equipment, and so on of the company — and see them in person. This won't always be possible, of course, but it's worth a try. You may think that this would be an intrusion. But don't let that put you off. Call the public relations department of the company (at times, this department might also be called the investor's relations department), and ask for a tour of the premises. For smaller companies that do not have such departments, call the vice-president of administration. You'll be surprised at how helpful most companies will be in trying to meet your request.

Then, when you go to the plant, have a careful look around. Is the place well kept? Does it give the impression that the company has money? Are the employees cheerful, or do they go about their chores in a state of gloom? (This, of course, would be an indication of productivity and labor relations.) Does the place look busy? Is there more office space than production space? And is the space being well used? You begin to get the idea: You're trying to get a feel for the health of the company, where its money comes from, where it goes, what its main lines of business are, and what is important to the company and what is not.

Next, you should have a chat with the people in management. They are only too happy to talk with serious investors. After all, most of them have stock or stock options, so if the stock becomes popular, the price will rise and their wealth will increase too. You may, if you like, mention that you are not the only one contemplating buying shares in the company. You have some friends who may follow suit. This would give you more clout. Then, have a talk with the company's suppliers and find out if the company pays on time or if it has cash problems. The company's customers, too, would be able to tell you if the company is aggressive in its marketing, whether it has a full line of products, whether it has recently introduced a new one. They would also tell you if the products are competitive, and if the displays are attractive.

If you feel really energetic, you could read in your local business library about the total industry. Here, you would be trying to find out where your company stands in relation to its competitors. Is it number one in the industry? Or number ten? Where is it heading? Has it recently increased its market share, or is it standing still? After a few days of such detective work, you'll begin to feel that you understand the business — as indeed you will. You could then try to forecast the impact of all kinds of developments on the performance of your company. With that knowledge, you would then be comfortable in holding the stock as a long-term investment, without losing sleep each time the market dips. Or you would know the dangers you should look for.

The second type of investment we'll describe here is the commodity contract. This is the prime security most people buy without even a minimal amount of research. Suppose you intend buying a futures contract for copper — that is, you believe the price of copper will rise more than is anticipated by the market, so that you can sell your contract for a profit. The contract will make you the proud owner of many thousands of pounds of copper. So you ought to know something about the metal.

First of all, then, you should go back to the library and pull out the *Encyclopaedia Britannica* and learn all you can about copper. Find out who wants it, what for, who supplies it, and in what quantities. This last factor is very important. You should find out which countries produce copper, how much they each produce, and how important the export of copper is to their economies. Suppose, for example, a major copper-producing country in Africa was in the throes of a revolution. Should you buy copper, sell it, or ignore it completely? Before you answer this, you would have to know how much of the world's copper is supplied by this particular country, whether lasting shortages would develop, how large the world's inventories are, and so on. You would have to know the market.

Similarly, if you read that fibre optics would make all copper in communication obsolete, should you immediately sell copper short? Again, you couldn't answer this question without understanding the market. If you checked it out, you would find that only 3%-5% of all the copper that's produced is used in communications. So even if this market for copper were declared obsolete, the impact would not be as significant as might be assumed without the benefit of research.

Knowledge, therefore, can make you money — and save you money. Because the more you know, the better the chance you have for outguessing the market. The market, after all, is full of people who, unlike you, have not done their homework. As you can see, an understanding of the fundamentals is what you should be aiming for. Only when you understand what is important and what is peripheral can you begin to develop a gut feeling for investment. This is the feeling we talked about earlier — and it is a feeling that all successful investors have.

Financial Statements: reading between the lines

In our last discussion on research, we blithely said that before you invest in a stock you should examine the issuing company's financial statements. This is undoubtedly true. You *should* look at these statements, study them carefully and draw some worthwhile conclusions on whether or not the stock is really worth buying. Unfortunately, most investors do not do this — for the good and simple reason that they do not fully understand how to interpret the myriad statements, figures, notes, and so on that companies are obliged to include. If you've ever been puzzled by a financial report — and, as we said, most investors have — you're probably not reading it properly. And that means if you go ahead and invest in the company anyway, you are likely taking an unnecessary risk. To avoid that possibility, let's try to dispel some of the mystery that corporate accountants like to cloak themselves in.

First of all, a company's financial statement consists of three sets of numbers: the balance sheet, the income statement and the statement of funds. These three schedules are enough to allow you to form an opinion about the quality of the company and its operations. So how do you interpret them?

Even without becoming a full-fledged financial analyst, there are several simple rules that you can learn. The first is an easy, but perhaps surprising, one: Annual reports should be read backward. Like books in Hebrew, they should be read from right to left. You should therefore start with the auditor's statement — usually printed at the very end of the report. Read it carefully, and look for any words of caution that these very prudent gentlemen may have inserted into their bill of health. Any such cautionary note is called "a qualified statement" in accounting parlance, and it amounts to saying that you buy into the company's shares at your own risk.

Your next step is to read the notes to the financial statements, in particular looking for any warnings and special treatments. Watch particularly for special gains and special losses: They would indicate that this year's performance may not be indicative of the company's usual performance. Then you go to the financial statements themselves — the balance sheet, the income statement and the funds statement. Let's look first at the balance sheet. It is really a snapshot of the company's holdings at a given point in time — usually at the end of a fiscal period (either year-end or the end of a quarter). It contains two sections: assets and liabilities.

The assets section is a schedule of the physical holdings (assets) of the company — cash, marketable securities (stocks and bonds), inventories, notes receivable (that is, money owed by customers), real estate, machinery and equipment, and so on. Aside from all these tangible assets, you may also find some intangible assets: patents, trademarks, and the like. The assets themselves are listed in two loose categories: short-term ("current") assets, and all other assets (fixed assets, investments, and the like). The assets schedule tells you just how much property (tangible and intangible) the company owns. To find out how much actually belongs to the shareholders and how much is yet to be paid for, you go to the second section of the balance sheet: the liabilities.

This section is also divided into three: short-term liabilities ("current liabilities"), all other liabilities of the company (long-term debt, taxes payable, and so on), and equity. This last one is the portion of the company's wealth that belongs to the shareholders. As an aside, we may remark that equity is lumped in the balance sheet under "liabilities," although strictly speaking liabilities are only the obligations of the company to persons and entities other than the shareholders. This means the term "liabilities" may include both debt and equity, as we've indicated above, or debt alone. You should check to see which alternative applies.

Summing up: The assets section gives you a breakdown of the physical composition of the property. The liabilities section details the legal ownership of all this wealth. It is small wonder that, by definition, total assets equal total liabilities when the shareholders' equity is included under the liabilities. In other words: Assets = Liabilities + Equity. Or, to express that another way: Equity = Assets-Liabilities. This applies to individuals as well as to corporations, and can be seen more clearly when applied to individuals.

For example: Suppose you have $5,000 in the bank as your total cash assets, and you have $10,000 invested in a home that is worth $50,000. What would your balance sheet look like?

Assets:	Current assets:	$5,000
	Fixed assets (house):	$50,000
	Total assets:	$55,000
Liabilities:	Long-term debt (mortgage):	$40,000
Equity:	Assets-liabilities:	$15,000

These are the basics of the balance sheet. And in theory they are really quite simple.

Now for the particulars: You will notice that the first line in the assets schedule of a financial report is the "current assets" (sometimes broken down even further into cash, inventories, and so on). This sum includes, in effect, all assets that can be turned into cash on very short notice. The liquidity of the company (the adequacy of the current assets) is a very good indication of the company's ability to stay in business: A company without enough cash in the till to pay its bills is in default on its obligations. This situation usually results in a noisy creditors' meeting, the result of which is an auction of the company's illiquid, or fixed, assets. The cash thus raised will be used to pay the bills and the debts.

How great should the liquid assets of a company be? Look under the section marked "current liabilities." These are the ongoing obligations of the firm: payroll, payments to suppliers, payment of interest on long-term debt, and so on. You should then compare current assets with current liabilities. If current assets are greater than current liabilities, then the firm can meet its ongoing obligations and all is well. Sometimes, the difference between these two amounts is computed. This difference is the working capital — that is, the money available for the ongoing operations of the company, as opposed to the money invested in plant and equipment, for example. At other times, the ratio of current assets to current liabilities (also called "current ratio") is calculated. If this ratio is below 1.0, the company is in danger of turning bellyup. If the ratio is between 1.5 and 2.5, the company is well managed in terms of its cash. If the ratio is too high — say, above 3.0 — then you may start suspecting that the management is too prudent, and, as a result, perhaps missing some opportunities.

The other type of obligation a company may undertake is the long-term debt. This has to be "serviced" in two ways: Interest charges have to be paid, and periodical repayments of principal have to be made (in the same way you have to "service" your mortgage). Obviously, the less debt the company has, the less vulnerable it is to bankruptcy in case of a recession, downturn in the economy, loss of a contract, or any other event leading to a decline in the cash inflow. On the other hand, a company with no debt at all operates only on the owners' capital, and is probably not taking advantage of all the opportunities available to it. Stated differently: With the same equity base, the owners could make a higher profit by borrowing and using other people's money. What then is the "best" debt ratio for a company? (This ratio may conveniently be calculated as the ratio of long-term debt to owners' equity.) Naturally, you would like the company to make as much profit as possible and borrow to the limit. Yet, you would not like it to operate with borrowed money exclusively, as the risk of bankruptcy would be too great. There is no fast rule here. Banks operate with extremely high debt ratios (because of something called "matching of assets and liabilities"), while companies in cyclical businesses (such as mining firms) have to be more conservative — otherwise, at a downturn, they would go broke. The best way to obtain an indication of the health of a company's financial structure is to compare it with similar companies in similar businesses, so that you get a feel for the adequacy of its finances.

Let us now say a few words about the equity section of the balance sheet. The owners' equity is also called, at times, the net worth, or the book value, of the company. As mentioned, it is the difference between the total assets and the total obligations of the firm. However, you must remember that the book value does not always correspond to the market value or even to the break-up value of the company. One of the most obvious reasons for this is the undervaluation of assets sometimes shown on the balance sheet. If assets are kept on the books at "historical costs" — inflation being what it is — the value of those assets may be greater now (in current dollars) than the original purchase price would indicate. This is especially true for non-depreciable assets such as land, timber-land, or oil and gas acreage not yet explored.

Now let's have a look at the income statement. It is a report describing, in a stylized form, how the assets listed in the balance sheet are put to work to augment the net worth of the shareholders. Stated differently, the income statement describes how profit is being generated by employing the assets. The details of the income statement can be broken down into categories. The basic ones are the revenues and the expenses. The net difference between these two is the net income (also sometimes called the net profit). Open a number of annual reports and compare the income statements. No two of them will be the same, since the types of revenues and expenses of different firms are almost always different. Even the same company may have new items appearing on its statement if the business has changed materially during the statement period. However, all income statements have many things in common, among them several recurring types of expenses and revenues (also called sales).

Revenues may be classified as operating revenues and non-operating revenues. The first covers all payments for services and products sold to customers, while the second may include items such as interest income on idle cash. Expenses may also be divided into categories. There are the fixed expenses, such as interest payments, which do not vary no matter what the level of sales or revenues; and there are the variable expenses, which may fluctuate as the sales level increases or decreases. The fixed expenses are, at times, also called overhead. In the income statement they are broken down into several items, such as rent, office expenses, and so on. Variable expenses are also given in detail: cost of goods sold, selling expenses, administrative expenses, and the like. The bottom line (the net profit) is the difference between the revenues and expenses. However, you should recognize that the net profit reported on the income statement is an accounting term, and does not always correspond to the cash profit you may have considered as the logical choice for an indicator of the firm's financial health. (The cash profit is the difference between the inflows and outflows of cash.)

For example, the depreciation charges, which are treated as an expense item on the income statement, are an imaginary deduction from the revenues. This works as follows: Suppose there is a machine of some kind that generates the bulk of the revenues of the firm. The life expectancy of the machine is ten years, and after ten years a new machine must be bought. Each year, therefore, one tenth of the cost of the machine will be deducted from the revenues as depreciation charges (called "straight line" depreciation) to give an indication of the "true" level of profit. Yet in cash terms, you would have to add back the depreciation charges in order to arrive at the true cash profit for the year. Of course, this cash will have to be plowed back into the business at the end of the tenth year, when the new machine is bought. But when that happens, you will not see the capital expenditure item on the income statement. You could see it on the balance sheet by inference: Cash balances would be reduced by the amount of the purchase, and "machinery and equipment" (on the assets side) would be augmented by the value of the new machinery purchased.

Similarly, if a debt is paid by a company (repayment of principal), you will not find any sign of it on the income statement, except through the reduction of interest payments on the (now smaller) outstanding debt. The balance sheet, too, will only show the reduction, not the direct payment made. The funds statement, on the other hand — the third of the financial statements — will specify exactly how much was paid to reduce the debt, how much was paid out in dividends, how much was spent on new machinery, and so on. In short, the funds statement is a schedule of the sources and application of cash. (It is sometimes called a statement of sources and uses of funds.) It is designed to give you the full picture of where cash comes from in the business, and where it goes within the business. Whenever you study financial statements, you should always remember that not all the items noted there are cash items, and that most non-cash items are a matter of judgment on the part of management, the auditors, or both. The funds statement is therefore very helpful for the understanding of the flow of "real" money in the business — that is, cash.

All three financial statements — the fund statement, the income statement and the balance sheet — are tied together in various ways. First of all, the net income as reported in the income statement is added to the retained earnings line in the balance sheet, to augment the net worth (after dividend payment is deducted). That is, the profit retained in the business after payment of dividends causes an increase in the net worth of the owners. Note that this net increase in the net worth, or book value, of the firm does not include any appreciation in the market value of the assets of the firm, or a depreciation. When such an "accounting recognition" is given to an appreciation or a depreciation, a "write-up" or a "write-down" of the assets results. This may occur because of an appreciation in the assets' value on the market (inflationary profit), or because of an unexpected drop in the market value of, say, securities held by the company.

Note that any changes in the book value of the company, for whatever reason (profit, loss, accounting changes or value on the market), first have to appear on the income statement. These changes may be in the nature of ordinary profit (or loss), or extraordinary profit (or loss). In other words, all changes in the company's book value first flow through the income statement.

According to many financial analysts, the funds statement is the second most important schedule (after the balance sheet). From the funds statement, you can learn just how much of the money generated by the business was earned in the actual business itself — that is, as receipts from customers, in investments, and so on — and how much was "earned" in, say, government subsidies or tax rebates. In the same way, you can see just how the money was spent — how much cash was invested in plant and equipment that will generate future profits (the machinery of our previous example), how much was used to repay old debt, how much was spent on research and development, and how much was taken out of the business in the form of dividends. But most important, you will see how the cash needs of the firm were met by the cash generated internally (that is, operating profit before depreciation and other non-cash items), and how they were met from money obtained from outside sources (borrowing, equity issue, and so on).

Obviously, a company that generates most of its cash needs internally is to be preferred to a company that has to rely on outside suppliers of capital. Sooner or later all outside suppliers of capital will demand their money back. Lenders will want interest and repayment of principal, and equity investors will want to be repaid in dividends. There will therefore be less money available for investments in machinery and productive facilities that will earn profits in the future. Companies that generate most of their own cash are therefore good "buys" in general. There are some companies that generate more cash than they need in the current business. In investor's parlance, these companies are called "cash cows." Their cash may be repaid to investors in the form of dividends, used for acquisitions, or employed to repay debt. All these uses of cash make for a higher share price, and for a happier investor. Look, therefore, for companies with a healthy generation of cash, and for ones that invest this cash in productive facilities.

Now, once you have grasped the purpose of the three financial statements, you may start doing some basic financial analysis. The net profit, when divided by the net worth, will give you the "book" return on equity of the company, or the return on investment of the company as related to its value on the books. In these inflationary days, anything less than about 14% or 15% is just not good enough. The "inverse" of this figure (that is, the book value, or net worth, divided by the net profit) is the "book multiple." It shows at what multiple of income (total or per share) the company is valued on its books (again, total or per share). Stated differently, this can also be seen as the number of years you'll have to hold the stock (at a constant level of profit) in order to have the company earn the price you paid for that stock (that is, if the company was all yours and you took out all the profit, how many years you would have to own it in order to obtain a "payback," in accounting parlance). Obviously, the higher the return on equity, and the lower the multiple, the better the stock.

The price of the stock on the market — and its market multiple — can be very different from the values you compute from the financial statements. This happens when the market assumes the company's prospects are not accurately represented by the latest available financial information. For instance, recent discoveries of gas in acreage held by a company may push up the real value of its assets — or, to express that differently, the market may value the potential for future profit of the company at a much higher level than is indicated by the current year's net profit.

Earlier on in our discussion, we computed several ratios from the balance sheet: debt to equity ratio, current ratio, and so on. You may do the same using data provided by the income statement and the funds statement. Thus, you may obtain margins by dividing expense items (or profit items) by the revenues. These figures (in per cents) will tell you just how much of a company's revenue is spent on each item of expense, and how much is left for profit. Any changes in these figures from one year to the next will draw your attention to a potential change (adverse or otherwise) in the business.

Remember: The "numbers" analysis does not provide you with the total answer to the question: Is this stock a good buy? However, it does provide you with questions you should ask yourself before investing. Every change in magnitude, margin or ratio, must have an explanation. Financial analysis will not tell you what that explanation is, but it will draw attention to the areas of the company's operations that you should study in closer detail.

Evaluating Management: is there a s.o.b. in the woodwork?

We will assume that, if you have managed to work your way through our discussion on annual reports, you now have a reasonable understanding of the "numbers" — the assets, liabilities, expenses, cash flows, net profits, and so on. There is, however, a lot more information in an annual report than just the numbers — and it's a lot easier to extract and understand. Also, it can be highly significant in determining your investment decisions.

Now we don't want to downplay the importance of the numbers. As we pointed out, before you invest you do want to know how much money the company owes, how much it is worth "on the books," how much it pays out in dividends, and so on. But at the same time, don't forget that it is the people in the company who make the business go. It is the managers and the directors who turn the fuzzy business prospects and opportunities into hard numbers with dollar signs in front of them. So, if you watch them, you may learn a lot about the future of the company — and the price of its shares.

Specifically, what should you watch for? First and foremost, you should look for change. As in an analysis of the numbers, an analysis of the people and the company is best started through a study of change. This is why the annual report can be important: It will tell who or what has changed. Unfortunately it probably won't tell you why the change was made. As with the numbers, you will likely have to find that out for yourself. But at least the annual report will tell you what to look for.

For example, the first and most important thing to look for is a change in the company's auditors. This is a rare event, but it does happen. And when management kicks out its own watchdogs, you had better watch out. This is a danger signal. It could mean something is radically wrong with the company and its stated financial strength. Next, you should look for changes in the top management. Has the chairman changed? The president? If so, why? And how long was he/she in place? Watch, also, for too-frequent shifts in management. This usually means the top people are not being allowed to do the job for which they were hired. Someone powerful is holding the company in a stranglehold. True, it might also mean that there were three or four incompetents in a row, and all had to be let go. But then, who has been so consistently hiring so many incompetents?

CBS is a case in point. William Paley is the controlling shareholder of this U.S. television network, and he recently fired his third or fourth president in the last six years (we'we lost count). Rumor has it that Paley does not fire his presidents because they fail. He fires them because they succeed. And no one at CBS is allowed to outshine Paley. You can bet that this kind of treatment of the top management people does not lead to a sparkling financial performance. Some investors actually short stocks such as this.

You should next watch for changes in the ranks of

the vice-presidents. If there is a very rapid turnover in one particular position, it might mean that no matter who holds the job, he or she will run into trouble. This could be another warning sign for you. Such a case is the one of Gulf + Western, where the position of vice-president for public relations is equipped with a revolving door. It is just possible that Chuck Bluhdorn (G + W's chief) has a number of dubious deals under his hat, which the PR vice-presidents find hard to accept. Equally, it could just mean that Bluhdorn is a tough master. Both cases might mean trouble for the stock, if there is too much turnover among the executives.

Sometimes the turnover is rampant among *all* categories of vice-presidents. If this is the case, it normally implies that the chief of the company is a mean s.o.b., and that, even with high salaries and fat perks, he cannot keep good people. This always means trouble. Such was the case of the First National Bank of Chicago, where the chairman, Robert Abboud, a hook-nosed ex-marine in elevator shoes, caused the resignations of almost 200 executives. Needless to say, the shares of the bank did not glow in the stock market. The stock of the bank is still depressed. But a kindly old uncle named Ben Heinemann has taken over the reins, and he is all milk and honey and light. You can bet that the price of the shares will soon reflect that change.

So much for people watching. But for those of you who like to take a more active approach to investing, you can go a lot further. We all know the value of inside information. The only problem is, it is hard to come by. However, if you watch your annual reports to find the executives who were fired, dismissed, or otherwise done in, you may gain an important source of inside information. How? By calling them, that's how. Many of those shafted by the mean s.o.b. at the top would just love to tell you their story. Of course, you would have to take it all with a grain of salt, and discount the adjectives and the undeleted expletives. But you can take a careful note of the hard facts, and draw your own conclusions.

Once you have talked to the executives who were let go, look back at the annual report and check out the stakes of the ones remaining. Look for the percentage of shares held by each of the managers. If this information is not in the annual report, you can find it in shareholder's circulars, prospectuses, and other company statements. This tells you who has a say in the company. But it doesn't tell you how competent those major shareholders are. This is something you might have to dig out for yourself — by researching their backgrounds. Most of the time, this information is given in short biographies published by the company. But you should also look in publications such as *The Canadian Who's Who* and in other relevant literature. Make a note of the manager's relative strengths and weaknesses.

If you have done your homework by analyzing the company properly, you may also have some idea about its future requirements for management talent. You can then compare these requirements with the available management resources — to see if there is a match. For example, if you see that the company has lost much of its market share recently, you may suspect, not unreasonably, that what it needs is marketing talent. But you might also see from the annual report that the board is made up of five engineers and six accountants, and all of them have large chunks of voting shares. Should you invest in such a company? Or should you sell the stock short?

Another simple test to apply is the name test. How many of the managers and directors have the same family name? It is possible that the two Browns on the board are not related. But five Gandolfos are just too much of a coincidence. You may then suspect that at least some of them did not gain their positions by merit alone. An example of this is the Schlitz beer company in the U.S. Its board teems with Schlitzes, who meddle with the company no end. There are always at least two conspiracies going on. Many young Schlitzes go to business schools and come back with MBAs. They want to have a say in the company. Older Schlitzes want to contribute on the basis of their rich life experience. The result? High turnover of top management and loss of market share to Miller. So again: Should you invest? Or should you go short?

A conflict on the board is not automatically bad, however. Sometimes you can see the fresh buds of a tender offer, if you look carefully. As you may know, many U.S. corporations have begun to buy chunks of other companies "as an investment." And what better way to buy a company than to take a small initial bite? You buy, say, 5% or 10%, put your man or woman on the board, learn the business, and then, after a few months, or even years, you tender for the rest of the shares from a point of real knowledge.

Obviously, once the acquiror tenders for the shares, he does so at a premium above the market. It would not be a bad idea if he bought the shares from you. The problem is that the lists of companies that have taken positions in other companies' stocks are well publicized. They are printed in *Barron's, Business Week* and *Forbes*, among others. Share prices, therefore, quickly reflect any sign of a potential takeover. So it's hard to get ahead of the market. However, this applies mainly to U.S. companies taking positions in other U.S. companies. What about the European companies? Many of them are buying into U.S. companies, and their purchases are not as widely publicized. They do, however, show up in annual reports.

For example, a German holding company called Bisping Capital recently bought 13.1% of the shares of Bangor Punta, a U.S. company holding Piper Aircraft, Smith & Wesson, and Lonestar Industries. Once it became clear that Bisping was preparing to tender for the rest of the shares of Bangor Punta, Bangor Punta's management called up the German company and a flurry of talks ensued. The result? A representative of Bisping — Ferdinand Graf von Galen (a youthful mustachioed German nobleman) — joined the Bangor Punta board. In exchange, Bisping gave its solemn word not to attempt a takeover before May 1, 1984. But what happens on May 2, 1984? Well, your guess is as good as ours.

Also, when a large company takes a position in another to the tune of many dozens (or perhaps hundreds) of millions of dollars, you can bet it has completed the best research that money can buy. You can also bet that the future of the "target" company, if not positively rosy, is at least secure. So annual reports can be a great source of information, not just to confirm that the stock you're interested in really is worth buying, but to help you identify which stocks you should be buying into in the first place.

Finally, let's say a brief word about the best place to get annual reports. There are three main ways you can do this. And they're all free. The first is to call the company that issues the annual report you're interested in. It will be happy to send a copy to you in the mail. You can also find annual reports in most libraries, at least for the major industrial corporations. Unfortunately, you won't be able to get U.S. annual reports this way; and you will have to go to a central library, not a local branch. Thirdly, you can collect your own annual reports, using the financial media as your prime source. You have probably seen — in the Toronto *Globe and Mail* for example (or in *Barron's, Forbes, Business Week* and other business publications) — full-page advertisements for annual reports that you can send away for. Usually, you just put a tick beside the annual reports you want, and send in your name and address (no money) and you receive your annual reports within a week or two. This is the best approach, since you can get as many reports as you want, with very little effort on your part.

Setting Your Goals: pausing before the plunge

If you're ever going to succeed at anything, it goes without saying that you have to know exactly what your goals are — and how you're going to reach them. This is as true of your personal investment program as it is of anything else, and although it may sound obvious, it's something that too many people too frequently overlook.

Goals vary, of course, depending upon the individual, and depending upon each individual's changing situation. But in broad terms, what we're all trying to achieve is that elusive something called financial security. For a fortunate few, financial security comes easily. Maybe you are lucky enough to have wealthy parents. Or maybe win a lottery or make a chance investment that earns you a fortune. For most of us, though, financial security is something we have to work for. One good thing, however, is that if you start early enough, the odds are in your favor. Financial security, and even wealth, are within your grasp — but only if you know how to go about achieving them. There are thousands of people in Canada who, in their working lives, will earn in excess of half a million dollars. The way they manage that money will determine whether they face luxury or poverty, an affluent retirement or a hand-to-mouth existence. The key, in other words, is effective personal financial management.

Management is basically any system you devise to ensure the proper sequencing of decisions — one that makes certain you do "first things first." It usually involves a series of activities such as planning, organizing, implementing and evaluating. For example, before you take your vacation, you first plan where you are going, how you will get there, how much money you will spend, where you will stay, who is going with you, and so on. Second, you organize; that is, you do all the things you have to do before you can go on your vacation, such as buying your air or rail tickets, repairing your car, making hotel reservations and buying clothes. The next step is implementation — in this case, actually going on your vacation. Sometimes, you will stick to your original plan, but at other times you will not. Perhaps the weather is poor, you find you don't like the destination you chose, or maybe you just come upon something else that you would rather do. The last step in the process is evaluation. Was it worth it? Would you go again? What would you do differently? Did you have enough money? Would you spend it in the same way? Notice, however, that this management process is circular, because your evaluation should get plugged in to your next planning cycle, if you want to be certain that you learn from your experiences.

The management process is much the same, whether you apply it to vacations or to your personal financial affairs. The basic contrast is that you are making different kinds of decisions. A vacation involves a relatively small amount of money compared with the funds involved in securing your future. Also, vacations come only once a year for most of us, while your paycheque comes at least once a month, and if you have other income, your investment activities might require your attention even more frequently. To take advantage of opportunities as they arise, you must know what you are doing. As we said, it is a simple fact of life that if you don't know where you want to go, you won't recognize your destination even if you arrive at it. The first step to financial security, therefore, is to devise an achievable, realistic plan that identifies where you want to be in, say, three to five years' time, and how you plan to get there.

What do you need to prepare such a plan? Let's take a look:

1. Your current position. You need financial statements for yourself; that is, a balance sheet showing your assets, liabilities, and net worth — simply a statement of what you have and what you owe, at current market values. A series of such balance sheets would show your progress at yearly (or shorter) intervals. Your banker uses one every time you obtain a loan, to ensure that he has sufficient security to cover your debt. You also need an income and expenditure statement to show where your funds for investment will come from, how large they will be, and when you will receive them.

2. Your investment alternatives. You must know the kinds of investments that are available, which will achieve your objectives and carry the type of risk you are prepared to accept. (This does not mean that you have to evaluate all investments; that is an impossible task.) Basically, there are only three kinds of investments. They can be grouped according to the objectives they are designed to achieve:

* Protection of capital: This type of investment is designed to make sure that the funds you invest are returned to you, and to provide you with a small level of income in the interval. This group includes Canada

Savings Bonds and guaranteed investment certificates.

* Income: This group of investments is designed to provide you with income, either for reinvestment or to cover your living expenses. It includes bonds, preferred and common shares of blue-chip companies, mortgages, some forms of real estate, and annuities.
* Growth: This type of investment is designed to offer an increase in market value over time. This group includes growth stocks, some types of real estate, and many speculative types of investment such as raw (underdeveloped) land, "penny" mining stocks, stock options, commodity and currency speculations, and so on.

3. How will your investment program be financed? How much will come from savings of your earned income? How much will come from investment income? How much can you afford to borrow for the purchase of investments? Is it profitable to borrow? All of these questions need answers, so your plan must include a "cash flow," indicating when the money will come in and when it will have to be paid out.

4. Income tax considerations. You will have to learn to make the Income Tax Act work for you instead of against you. This means evaluating all investments on an after-tax basis. What is important is not so much your gross income, but what you have left after you've paid taxes.

5. Special constraints on your investments. Do you want funds available for your children's university education? Are you saving to buy a cottage? Or a larger home? All of these factors will affect what you invest in, and at what yield.

After you have considered the above points, you will be in a position to start drawing up your plan. It may seem like a lot of work. And it is, particularly the first time. But subsequent revisions will be relatively simple. The important thing to remember is that if you don't look after your own financial security, no one else will. First of all, you are the one who has to live with the consequences of your actions. Secondly, it is to your benefit to manage your money effectively.

If, for example, you can manage to save $2,000 per year, on the average, over a 30-year working career, and if you invest that money at an after-tax rate of 8% per year, then at retirement you will have $226,500. If, however, you can, by effective management, increase your average savings to $2,500 per year, and your effective after-tax yield to 9% — relatively modest changes — then you will end up with $340,700. That is an increase in capital of $114,200 and an increased annual income from that capital of about $13,000 per year. In other words, even a small increase in the amount of money you have available for investment, and a small increase in the yield you get on that money, can be highly significant in the long run. That's why money management is so important.

Let's assume that you have established a plan showing such things as your current financial status, the amount of money you have available for investment purposes, and the financial goals you want to attain in the next five years. You are now in a position to start picking the specific investments that will allow you to meet your objectives. Right away, however, you will be faced with the problem of over-choice that we mentioned earlier. There are so many different investment opportunities that it is not possible to evaluate them all. Somehow, you have to find a way of reducing the choice to manageable proportions. The only way you can do this is to have some orderly means of selection firmly established in your mind before you begin the search.

For example, you might feel that you should set up

an emergency fund of some kind — money that is immediately available at any time you might suddenly need it. You can keep this emergency money in a savings account at a bank or trust company, or perhaps in something like Canada Savings Bonds. They will usually give you a higher yield, but they are just as secure and liquid as a savings account. Your first decision, therefore, would be to determine how large your emergency fund should be. It is important that you do this now, not when you are actually faced with the emergency. As a guideline, many people set aside about three to six months' net income in their emergency fund.

Having settled that question, your next step is to decide how to invest your remaining available funds. And the way to do this is to determine your priorities. As we said, there are really only three kinds of investment objectives you can have: protection of capital, income and growth. You should decide which one of the three is most important, and which is least important. Clearly, you don't have to commit all your funds to the pursuit of a single objective: You can choose any balance you like.

For example, if your income needs are already fully satisfied, you might want to concentrate on growth and perhaps capital protection. But if you now have an inadequate amount of money coming in, you might want to emphasize income as your immediate objective. As a general rule, if you are looking for capital protection or income, you should consider bonds and preferred and common shares of blue-chip companies. If you are primarily interested in growth, you might want to look at common shares of non-blue-chip companies, or at such things as underdeveloped land, which have the potential for a large increase in value. Usually, the greater potential for growth, the lower the income and the degree of capital protection. However, investing for growth gives you the best chance of protecting yourself against inflation.

Your next move is to decide how much money you are prepared to put into any one investment, no matter what that investment is. Again, this will help narrow your choices. If, for example, you are prepared to invest a maximum of $2,000 in any one company, then you will be limited to buying bonds or common and preferred shares up to a value of about $20 (since shares are normally traded in lots of 100). The degree of risk you are prepared to accept will play a part in this decision. If an investment is particularly risky, you should probably allocate it only a small percentage of your total capital. Also, by limiting the amount of money you are prepared to commit to any one investment, you will be able to spread your investment around. This will reduce your risk because you will not have all your investment eggs sitting in one basket.

Only when you have considered all these points — and answered them to your own satisfaction — will you be in a position to find the investments that you think will meet your financial objectives. Suppose, as an example, your financial plan calls for you to be able to save $15,000 over the next five years, and that you already have set up an adequate emergency fund. You may decide that you want to put 50% of your money into income-generating investments, and the maximum single investment you are prepared to make will be $2,500. You may also decide that on this group of investments you are prepared to accept a yield/risk level of, say, 12% per year before tax. You may then elect to put the remaining 50% of your money into growth investments, with a maximum single investment here of $1,500. You may also feel you should expect a return from this group of investments of not less than 25% per year before tax. At this point, you are in a position to "zero in" on those investments that will meet these specific objectives, and to eliminate all others that will not. You have, in other words, narrowed your choices to manageable proportions. (We emphasize, however, that the example here is purely illustrative; it is not necessarily the course you should follow.)

Some other points are worth considering here. First, always evaluate your investments on an after-tax basis. The most important figure to keep in mind is your marginal income tax rate; that is, the percentage of tax you will pay on the next dollar you earn. If, for example, your marginal rate is 40%, you will only get 60 cents out of any dollar increase in salary or interest income. But if you earn a capital gain at that marginal tax rate, you will be able to keep 80 cents out of the dollar. And if you earn dividend income, you will be able to keep 85 cents out of the dollar. This is because interest, capital gains and dividends are taxed at different rates, with the taxes on dividends and capital gains being considerably lower than on interest, as we will see later. As a result, you may actually want to have a lower before-tax yield, if it leaves you with more money in your pocket after you've paid your taxes.

Also, keep in mind the advantages of tax shelters, since they allow you to invest pre-tax dollars — always more than after-tax dollars — with the result that your return can be substantially increased. (We'll have more to say about this later on.) Bear in mind, too, the benefits of paying off your personal debts. This can often give you a high return on your money, and not involve any risk. If, for example, you have a mortgage on your house at, say, 12% and your marginal tax rate is 40%, then a prepayment on your mortgage — if allowed by the contract — will yield the same as an investment with a pretax yield of 20%. Such an "investment" guarantees your principal and gives you a high return. The only drawback is that the investment is not liquid: You cannot "sell" it unless you sell your house or refinance it.

Finally, in any financial planning and money management, you should always include some time for evaluation. Many people think that this is the most important step in any management process; it is also the least used. It is no sin to make a mistake. But it is a sin to make a mistake and then not correct it, or to make a mistake and not learn from it. Also, the marketplace is always changing, so change is the only constant. You have to keep abreast of new developments. The only reason for buying (or selling) an investment is what you expect it will do in the future, not what it has (or has not) done in the past. As a result, you should regularly review your portfolio to make sure that the reasons you made a particular investment are still valid. If they are not, then it is time for a change.

Managing Your Broker: who's he really working for?

Whenever you invest in the stock market, the one person you *always* have contact with is your broker. In spite of this, most investors, even seasoned ones, have at one time or another been confused about the relationship they have with their broker, and about what they can reasonably expect him to do. For example, depending upon the type of transaction you enter into with him, your broker may be dealing with you either as a principal or as an agent. There are important differences. Also, depending upon the relationship, the cost of doing business with him may be clear to you — or unknown.

Since the relationship is so important to the way you make many of your investment decisions, let's explore it in some detail. We'll look first at your dealings with him when he acts as a principal. Legally, in this situation, your position is one of equals dealing on *opposite* sides of a transaction. He buys, you sell; or he sells, you buy. A price is negotiated for the transaction and a deal consummated with all the legal aspects of a contract. There is no intermediary. Usually, the principal relationship occurs in two types of transactions — either bond trades or new issues of securities that have been underwritten by your broker's firm (either acting alone or in cooperation with other brokerage firms).

Let's look first at the bond trades. Suppose, as an example, that you wish to buy $10,000 par value of Government of Canada 9½% bonds due October 1, 2001, and the market is quoted 80½ bid to 81 asked. If you are a seller, you will receive 80½, or $805 per $1,000 par value. If you are a buyer, you will pay 81, or $810 per $1,000 par value. (Bond prices are quoted in relation to $100, although the trading unit is $1,000 par.) The trade is done on a principal basis — that is, you deal *with* your broker, not through him, and you are on *opposite* sides of the deal.

The spread is half a point, or $5 per $1,000 par value. If your broker buys from you at 80½ and immediately makes another principal transaction to sell at 81, he makes $5 profit. However, if he holds the bonds as inventory — that is, he "positions" the bonds — he could make more profit if the market rises. Conversely, if the market declines, he could lose money. Either way, though, the deal is concluded as far as you are concerned, but may or may not be as far as your broker is concerned.

So how much profit can your broker hope to make?

That depends on the spread between the bid price and the asked price, which will vary with the security being quoted. Short-term Canada bonds with less than one year to maturity may be quoted with a spread of a few cents only — for example 99.20 bid to 99.22 asked. This means $992.00 bid to $992.20 asked per bond for a difference of 20 cents per $1,000 par value. Up to three years in maturity, the spread could be 99.20 bid to 99.30 or 99.40 asked. Over three years in maturity, the quote would probably be 99⅛ to 99⅜ or 99 to 99½. Provincials and provincial guarantees such as Ontario Hydro, B.C. Electric, and so on, as well as municipal bonds, usually trade on half-point spreads. Corporate bond spreads usually range from one full point to as much as two, three or four points. As you can imagine, the more difficult it is to find buyers and sellers for the bond or debenture, the wider the spread your broker will call. He does this to protect himself against market swings that may take place while he attempts to find a new buyer or seller. He might have to wait minutes, hours, days, weeks or even months. These delays and risks will determine the profit he wants from the trade.

Bonds and debentures normally pay interest every six months, and interest accrues, or is earned, on a daily basis. The 9½% Canada bonds we mentioned above pay $47.50 per $1,000 par value on October 1 and April 1. If you bought these bonds on May 1, the seller would be entitled to the interest from April 1 to the date of settlement, May 8. (Settlement date is normally five business days after the transaction, or trade date.) This is 38 days from April 1, and represents $10.03 earned, or accrued, interest per $1,000 bond. And this interest belongs to the seller. If you, as the purchaser, hold the bond to the next interest payment date of October 1, you will collect *all* the interest from April 1 — in other words, $47.50 per $1,000 par value. Therefore, you receive interest for each day you have held the bonds. However, you have already put up $10.03 per $1,000 par value to pay the seller his accrued interest, and thus you are out the use of these funds until the interest payment date. If the number of bonds is substantial and the interest period has been running, say, five months, then the accrued interest could also be substantial. The loss of return on this accrued interest may cause the buyer to lower his bid price in compensation.

The other major principal relationship you will have with your broker involves new issue offerings. These represent underwritings, where a dealer syndicate has purchased new securities from the issuing government or corporation and offers them for resale to the public at a higher price. This is a liability transaction for your broker. He commits himself to purchase securities from the issuer at a specific price and on a specific day, regardless of market conditions.

For example, one recent new issue consisted of 4,950,000 Steel Company of Canada $25 par value convertible 7.76% preferreds. These were offered to the public at $25.00 net per share, with Stelco receiving $24.125 per share. However, the issue came out at the time of rapidly rising interest rates in March, 1980, and not all the shares were sold. When trading started in early April, it was around $23 per share. This means a loss of $1.125 per share to the underwriting syndicate for every share sold at this price. In contrast, TransCanada Pipelines on April 18, 1980 issued for settlement on May 6, 1980 an additional 3,200,000 shares from treasury. The price was $22 net per share to the public, although the outstanding stock was trading at $22¼ (plus commission) on the Toronto and Montreal stock exchanges. The company received $20.95 net per share, so the underwriter's gross profit was a healthy $1.05 per share.

The main point to remember, though, is that, in

this kind of transaction, your broker has a vested interest in selling you securities that his firm has helped to underwrite. This does not necessarily mean you shouldn't trust him if he suggests you buy a new issue — some new issues can be very profitable for both you and your broker. What it does mean, though, is that you are dealing here with another principal, one who is on the opposite side of the transaction from you. This is something you should bear in mind when listening to his proposals.

Now, let's look at the more normal "agency" relationship that you have with your broker. This arises when you buy and sell securities *through* your broker as opposed to buying them *from* him or selling them *to* him. Under these circumstances, your broker acts as your agent. He does what you do. So if you sell, he sells on your behalf, on the floor of the exchange where the stock is listed. The price he receives is what you receive—less his commission for the execution of your order. This commission is compensation for the facilities he provides for trading the stock, including the investment in membership on the exchanges, floor traders, delivery, transferring of the registration, and so on. These rates vary, as we'll see in a later discussion, when we will show you what the rates are — and how to reduce them. For now, though, the most important commission charge you should be aware of is the "turnaround commission rate reduction."

Basically, if you buy or short a listed security and reverse the position through the same broker within 45 calendar days of the settlement date of the original transaction, then the commission on the closing transaction may be reduced by *up to 50%*. Most brokers insist on this turnaround being requested and approved before the closing transaction is entered. Your broker will not deliberately avoid telling you about the turnaround, but he may have forgotten or not have bothered to check the time span. So it is up to you to check your settlement date and the 45-day limit when you turn around your shares. This could result in important savings for you.

So what can you expect your broker to do in return for his commission? Basically, if you are dealing with a full-service broker, you can expect:

* to be offered new issues when they are available.
* to obtain research material on general market conditions and specific securities.
* to receive opinions on specifically requested securities.
* to be able to deal in all markets and exchanges.
* to receive monthly statements.
* to receive transaction summaries on an annual basis.
* to receive a recapitulation of dividends and interest paid or received by your account on an annual basis.
* to receive portfolio evaluations monthly, quarterly, or annually.
* to have your securities held in safekeeping (a fee may be charged for this).
* to have dividends and interest collected in your account, if on margin.
* to be advised of news and changes affecting your security holdings.

In addition, there are many more services that your broker can, and will, provide, if your account and your relationship warrant it. If you're not getting them, complain — or immediately consider getting yourself a new broker.

Balancing Your Portfolio: a personality to match

So far in our discussion, we have mentioned that there are really only three investment objectives you might want to meet: protection of capital, income and growth. As we've said, there is no need for you to restrict yourself to just one of these objectives — and indeed, if you do, you will probably end up with a portfolio that is out of balance and not as good as it should be. So let's assume now that you are aiming for all three objectives. We'll assume, too, that you have set aside an emergency fund, and that you are investing only disposable income, rather than income you need to live on, since it is this disposable income that is the only money you should ever consider putting at risk. Where should you begin? How, in other words, do you build a balanced portfolio?

Well, since the first $1,000 of interest income, net of carrying charges, is tax-free, this makes your initial step simple and obvious: You should acquire sufficient debt instruments to obtain that $1,000 of interest income. At today's interest rates, this would require about $10,000 of capital. And you couldn't go far wrong if you put that capital into such debt instruments as government or blue-chip corporate bonds, or into bank or trust company guaranteed investment certificates (GICs) and short-term paper.

Once you have earned $1,000 of interest income, your next step in building a balanced portfolio should be to consider the purchase of some preferred shares. This is recommended because, as we have indicated elsewhere, the after-tax return from dividend income can be very attractive. And the net return on your capital plus your savings will allow you to compound your investment and thus achieve a higher capital formation rate.

Suppose you purchase preferred shares that yield 9% and suppose, too, that you are a resident of British Columbia whose taxable income is over $25,284. This would give you a federal rate of 32%, and a B.C. rate of 44% of the federal rate, or 14.08%, for a total marginal tax rate of 46.08%. In this bracket, $100 of dividend income, $1.589 of interest income and $1.105 of capital gain will each produce $0.847 of net after-tax income. So you can calculate that the 9% preferred dividend yield would give you 9% × 0.847 = 7.62% after tax. The interest income yield required to provide the same net after-tax would be 9% × 1.589 = 14.30%.

The immediate cash flow from your income dollars would provide you with an offset to possible capital gains in future dollars. It would be argued that inflation and declining purchasing power are not adequately covered by the income, but at least the income is more reasonably assured. Also, you can obtain some capital gain from preferred shares if interest rates decline. And, if you purchase convertible preferred shares, then the gain in the value of the common shares will reflect in the value of the preferreds.

How is your portfolio shaping up so far? It has its tax-free interest income, and a good net yield on preferreds, with some prospects for capital gain. Let's now look at the introduction of common shares into your holding. First, any common share you consider should have an easily obtainable market, and the spread between the bid and asked prices should be narrow — for example, it should be listed on the Toronto Stock Exchange and quoted at, say, 9½ bid to 9¾ asked. The market should also have reasonable depth. In other words, the purchase or sale of a fairly large number of shares should not move the market. The daily trading volume and the size of the bid and asked prices will indicate the depth of the market.

The common shares you select should be compatible with your personality and objectives. You should buy them on the basis of a number of factors: diversification of your portfolio by security type, industry, geographical location, and so on. Also, the earnings yield should be attractive, have demonstrated consistent, healthy growth, and be expected to maintain or increase that growth. You could also select common shares from your own business sources and assessment of the market. However, you should stay with broadly traded and well-known common shares. Try to add high-quality shares that have liquidity and marketability. They may not pay dividends but if they do, at least you can hold them if your timing of their puchase proves to have been wrong.

As your savings and reinvested funds expand, increased capital will allow you to add to your selections. Your purchases can become more aggressive. And you can begin to consider such specialized vehicles as options and warrants. Remember that you cannot expect to hit big winners, especially on your first try at the market. You have to take the slow and steady approach. And that's why you need a three- or five-year plan. We recommend that you do not hold too many securities in total. If you have more than fifteen, it becomes difficult to track market movements and your paperwork increases rapidly. Think of the cheques, quarterly statements, annual reports, T5s, T600s, and other records you would have to keep. You would start to become your own mutual fund, but without the benefits. As market conditions vary, then obviously the balance of your holdings can, and probably should, change. You might sell commons and move into cash to capitalize your profits. It is not necessary to swing from one common to another common; your mix of securities should vary with conditions.

In summary, take a long-range approach consistent with your means, age, health, responsibilities and objectives. Acquire your securities in a logical, organized, step-by-step manner. Buy bonds first for the tax-free interest; then preferreds for the net after-tax income and some prospect for capital gain; and finally, common shares for your aggressive fight against decreasing purchasing power.

The Stages of Man: countering the follies of youth

In our last discussion, we said that your investment strategy should change with your age and responsibilities. Let's now have a closer look at that idea, because it is one of the key factors that will help you decide how your portfolio should be arranged.

First, let's examine your investment lifetime and see how it breaks down. Basically, like your investment objectives, it can be divided into three, as follows:

1. Between the ages of 18 and, say, 30 (or 35), which is usually the period when you embark on work, family and/or career. Your income flow has not yet peaked, but your needs are large: You marry, buy a house, fill the house with the patter of tiny feet, and go to the Bahamas frequently to relax and escape from same.

2. Between the ages of 30 (or 35) and 55 (or 65), which is normally when your income peaks. You have probably stabilized in a career, so your income is not only greater than it was when you started, but it is also surer. This gives you what we shall call the "income safety net."

3. Beyond the age of 55 (or 65, depending on your retirement plans). You will be relying mainly on investment income (and pension benefits, which are the investment income of the pension funds). Your needs are only two: consumption, and provision for your family after you are gone.

In each of these three periods of your life you have different needs and different temptations for the use of your money. In the first period, for instance, you will probably be tempted to live it *all* up — especially after the successsful outcome of a particular investment coup you are proud of. This is something you should resist. Certainly, you should not live in want; but you should try not to consume *all* the investment income you earn. In this period in your life, you are better off investing all excess income for *future* benefits. Do not forget you are still young, and compound growth therefore works best now. In this period, too, you probably do not yet have high job security, so it would be a mistake to concentrate only on capital gains investments — the high-fliers that are also normally riskier. It is better to go for the less risky ones, and reinvest the income. And it would be even better if you could moonlight and generate still more income, and invest that too.

Naturally, some of your money should be left in a safe harbor — just in case. World wars, revolutions, being fired, and many other unforeseen disasters may suddenly strike. The proportion of your money to be put into safe investments — suggested in the table that follows later — is only a rough indication; but it should give you an idea of the required shift in your investment goals as your age advances.

And when you *do* age, you'll already have an important asset: the security of your job — either tenure in your place of work, or expertise that will make it easier for you to find new employment should the need arise. So in this, the second period in your life, you can afford to take higher risks. Do not forget you probably are worth more in this period of your life, after more than twenty years of working and investing. You should now invest more and more in capital gains investments — in investments that will bear fruit in the future at the expense of returns now: energy stocks, for instance, or highly leveraged real estate deals that have "zero cash flows," movie tax shelters, and so on. Your requirement for income has now stabilized, as you are probably settled down. Also, you have probably paid off most of the mortgage on your home. Isn't it time you spent a little on yourself? Well, don't splurge yet, but you may increase your income consumption a little. Also, you should not neglect to keep a certain proportion of your money in gold, cash, and other liquid forms of safe wealth. Some security is needed at all points in your life.

Finally, in your retirement years, you can begin to enjoy it all. You can now convert the growth stocks and the go-go funds you own into solid, income-producing investments: rental apartment houses, dividend-paying stocks (both common and preferred), or even high-grade convertible bonds (pure bonds are a folly in these inflationary days). You should also mix safety with income production, and to this end you may consider something like South African gold stocks. Some South African gold stocks — so-called Kaffirs — are in reality self-liquidating gold mines. They pay dividends of more than 15% in yield. This extraordinary rate is due to one simple fact: Most of the income of the mine is paid out to the shareholders, and little is retained to develop new gold prospects. (This, please note, is true only for the smaller mines; the larger ones pay smaller dividends, but are also more enduring.) The gold portion in your portfolio can of course consist of — instead of or as well as —

gold bars, gold funds, or any of the other forms of the gold now infesting the market.

Let us now look at the table, which shows the approximate percentages of the various investment goals at different times in your investment life:

Approximate age period	Investment goal		
	Income	Capital Gains	Safety
18-30 (35)	20%-30%	30%-40%	40%-50%
30 (35)-55 (65)	10%-20%	50%-60%	10%-20%
Above 55 (65)	30%-40%	20%-40%	30%-40%

You can see that the need for safety is greatest when you are young; then it tapers off, as you acquire the safety net of a job and some worldly assets; and then it begins to rise again when you are retired and no longer working. The composition of capital gains investments in your portfolio is quite large to begin with — of necessity (your home is a very large percentage of your wealth) — but you are trying to earn income that you can reinvest. Then you shift into more risky investments with a longer payoff, and finally, before you retire, you shift back into income-producing investments. Note that, even in your retirement, you still keep some of your assets in long-term capital gains investments. This is really the part of your money you intend to leave as your estate. Therefore, if you intend to provide for three former wives and seventeen teenage kids, you'd better increase the portion of capital gains investments in your holdings even when you approach senility. Of course, if you have no one you want to provide for, don't leave anything behind.

Finally, let us end on a word of caution: Never forget that there's no such thing as a sure thing. Even if you are *certain* that a particular investment is a surefire winner, never forget to leave a certain portion of your money in cash and its equivalents. Swiss banks talk a lot about the "10% gold insurance" — that is, leaving 10% of your money in gold or equivalents (they mean Swiss francs, or Swiss-franc denominated high-grade bonds). But do not increase this portion unduly either. If you hold too much cash (in Canadian dollars), inflation will slay you. If you buy too much gold, you may find you have bought it at $875 an ounce with food money. The main thing to remember is that no matter how lucrative an investment seems to you, always consider it in the context of your own investment plan — a plan that constantly changes as you grow older.

Timing: sorting out the good jokes from the bad

If you were to draw up a list of the most successful stock market investors — a kind of historical hall of fame — you would probably have to put J.P. Morgan, the late but largely unlamented American capitalist, close to the top of your list. He was so successful that, no matter where he went, people were always coming up to him, seeking his advice, asking which way he thought the market was going to move. Always, Morgan would give the same answer: The market is going to fluctuate. It will go up and it will go down. And the way to make money is to buy when it's down and sell when it's up.

Buy low, sell high. That maxim is as simple in theory as it is difficult to put into practice. How do you know when the market for a particular stock is down, and how do you know when it's up? Essentially, you never really do. Only when you look back at past performance can you see when the market for a stock was at a low (when you should have bought) and when it next reached a peak (at which time you should have sold). It's one of the most frustrating aspects of the market, that you only know exactly what is happening after it has happened. Even so, the appeal of the maxim remains. It is so logically simple and so self-evidently true that there must be some way in which it can be turned to advantage.

And there is. Because what the maxim is really talking about is timing. And timing — at least *good* timing — is one of the ways of bending the odds in your favor and giving a boost to your return on investment. You probably accept that what separates a good comedian from a mediocre one is not his material, but his timing. So it is in the stock market. We all have the same material to work with. As often as not, the difference between success and failure is the ability to get in and out of a stock at approximately the right time. (You can't expect to be completely and consistently accurate on your timing; the best you can hope for is to come close.) This, of course, is another one of those easier-said-than-done situations. It is extremely difficult to spot when a stock is at a low point, just due for a rise, and when it is at a high point, ready for a fall. Perhaps the only way to do it is to have inside information, or to be very familiar with the company behind the stock and to know what influences its performance. Unfortunately, having inside information is rare, and trading on it can be illegal. We are, therefore, left with the second choice: being very familiar with the company's affairs. The problem here is that there are so many companies that it is impossible to be familiar with them all, even superficially. But if you look at the performance of their shares, you'll find that all of them have in common the fact that, as J.P. Morgan said, their share prices fluctuate.

Even when the price of a share has been moving in one direction for a long time, following an upward or downward trend, there will still be fluctuations within that trend. And there will also be some evidence of long-term cycles. Even if the cycles occur over several years, they will still be there. Suppose, then, that you were to pick, say, just three or four large, stable and publicly traded companies — a bank, perhaps, a utility and maybe a mining company — companies that are easy to follow both in their affairs and in their stock market performance. Don't pick a conglomerate: Too many factors affect it, so that it is extremely difficult to determine which ones will dominate, especially when all are moving in different directions. But with just three or four companies to follow, you should soon become familiar with their affairs and with the forces that most affect them.

As an example, let's look at Bell Canada. Every now and then, Bell goes through the ritual of trying to get permission from the federal government to raise its rates. If the regulatory committee, in this case the Canadian Radio-television and Telecommunications Commission, refuses to grant an increase, then Bell shares may take a small- to medium-sized dip. Sooner or later, however, the story will end with the predictability of a Harlequin romance, and Bell will get an increase. At that point, the company's profit potential is seen to improve, and its share price likely moves up. If you were to study the sequence of events surrounding Bell's rate applications — as well as the way the government and the electorate react to those applications — and if you were to relate that sequence to the performance of Bell Canada shares, then you would likely find a correlation. And the next time Bell went seeking an increase, you would be able to predict with reasonable accuracy the immediate effect on the shares. That would substantially increase your chances of buying Bell Canada stock at an opportune moment, and also, of course, of getting back out at the most appropriate time. In other words, your timing would have been improved.

Now let's look at a mining company. Like all such companies that deal in commodities, the mines are sensitive to changing commodity prices. If the price of copper, say, goes into a slump, then copper mining companies will suffer too. Equally, if copper prices suddenly rise, then copper company shares will rise in tandem. As a rule, there is a cycle for every commodity. Copper happens to have a long one — about nine years on average — but other metals have cycles that are considerably shorter. By following these cycles, you can get a pretty good idea of when you should buy mining shares, and when you should sell them.

The key thing in all such situations is to find out which factors affect the price of a stock, and then to follow those factors, and the stock too, to see the best times to buy and to sell. Since, as we said, it is not possible to become intimately familiar with all the available companies and stocks, you have to pick just a few that you know you will be able to follow. You should find out who their directors and officers are. Follow their progress. Get to know their strengths and weaknesses. Find out what the company is planning, and when it is planning to do it. This means following newspaper reports on the companies you've selected, building up a file, consulting the business libraries for background information, and, as we have suggested elsewhere, talking to the company public relations departments to keep abreast of developments. It also means keeping an eye on the companies' shares and relating the price moves to the events you are following. Eventually, you will get a feel for the companies' operations and for the way their share prices move.

One key requirement for success, following this strategy, is a great deal of patience. You must be willing to wait, perhaps until next summer or fall, until the shares of that bank or that mining company you're following, have reached what you hope is an all-time low. Then you can buy. The main point, though, is that most people, when they consider investing, decide to put in some money at a particular point in time — and then they look around for the best stocks to choose. What we are suggesting here is that you pick your stocks *now* — the large, stable and publicly traded companies you've decided to follow — and then wait for the best time to invest. We don't suggest that you follow this strategy exclusively, but it is worth your while to pursue it, parallel to some of the other strategies you may decide to follow.

The Banana Peels: avoiding the traps for the unwary

In the world of investments, only results count. Intentions, even the best of them, don't bring you a consolation prize. As we have stressed, if you want your investments to succeed, the first thing you should do is establish your goal — that is, determine what results you want to achieve. Once you have done that, you should get defensive and recognize (and avoid) the more common errors into which most investors, at one time or other, fall.

Here, then, are some popular traps that you should sidestep. The first, and the most common, is ignorance — not knowing enough about the investment in which your hard-earned money is stored. You probably know people who shell out their money on the advice of a broker, or after hearing a tip from a friend. They buy hundreds, even thousands, of dollars' worth of stock, without once investigating the underlying company — something you should never do. A second mistake, and almost as common, is made by people who try to keep up with everything in the world of finance and investments. They try to learn all there is to know about the one investment in which their money is stored. And we mean *all* — every little detail. This is unnecessary, of course, and a dismal waste of time. Instead, you should try to distinguish between the important and the peripheral, between the major and the secondary. For instance, look at cash flow before you look at earnings; look at profit before you look at total assets. Try to develop an understanding of what's important — and ignore what's not.

A third error is panic. Buying or selling in a hurry is almost always a mistake (although at times, it may be necessary to remedy a previous error). If it is not done too frequently, there's no crime in that. But if you do it too often, then you are surely doing something wrong. In general, the *frequent* buying and selling of investments is another basic error. Every time you trade, it costs you money — in two ways. There's a spread between the bid and asked prices, both in stock and bonds. That's how the market maker (the floor trader) makes his living. Also, your friendly broker gets a hefty commission — about 2%-2½% in Canada — whenever you buy and sell. So if you trade too frequently, you are losing profit, and the only one who's gaining is your broker.

Let us now talk about diversification. You probably agree that your money is best kept in various investment baskets. But this isn't always true. If you have lots of money, by all means spread it around and so spread your risk. But if you are just starting out, with, say, only a few thousand dollars, then concentrate what you have to get the biggest bang. This doesn't mean you should put everything into one stock, but it does mean you should focus on a few areas only. When you are just starting out, you can't avoid taking a bigger risk. You may have to settle for less diversification than you would like, but if done within reason and after proper research, this is wholly appropriate.

Later on, once you've diversified, make sure you don't switch your eggs too quickly from one basket to another. This is one of the surest ways to break them. It is only natural that one of your investments will do better than the others. But don't sell everything else and put all your money into that one success. If you must acquire more of the winning investment, then shift some of your other dollars into it. (This is called averaging the cost of your investments, and is not a bad idea if done in moderation.) But never go for broke, unless you are willing to get there.

Another common, and related, error is holding on too long to a loser. This happens when you have illogically convinced yourself that an investment you have bought is going to increase in value. You've told yourself, your friends, and your family, that the investment is going to go up, and by God, you're going to hold on until it does. Now, though, you are investing for the growth of your ego, not for the growth of your money. In a word, don't. If a stock you have lovingly researched now goes down in a tailspin, sell it and chalk up your losses to experience.

This brings us to the next error — that of not keeping track of your investments. It is important that you keep track of all your trades. When did you buy an investment, at what price (net of commissions), and why? Also, when did you sell, at what price, and why? This gives you a cold-blooded record of your performance;

you will be able to see your total performance — not just the one or two coups that stick best in your memory.

Next, there's the error of gullibility, of believing your friends when they tell you that they have made a killing. Now maybe they have and maybe they haven't. But even if they can prove it, you shouldn't blindly follow their lead. What about their other investments? Why aren't they talking about those? No one is ever consistently right, and to assume that they are is to surrender your fate to someone else's folly. Also, you will probably develop unrealistic expectations, and start taking risks you would otherwise be unwilling to assume. This last point is valid not only for the boasting of your friends, but also for the boasting of advisers, newspapers, and analysts with specialized interests.

Say you read that an oil analyst claims oil stocks have tripled within a year (some have), or that a gold bug claims gold more than doubled in less than twelve months (it did). Should you go and invest in oil stocks and gold? Perhaps you should, but that conclusion is not automatic. You will be committing two errors if you think that it is. First, you will be assuming that if your own portfolio has not done as well as the top-performing segment in the market, then you have somehow failed. This is nonsense. Even if someone has made a lot of money, someone else has lost. If not, where did the winners get all the money they made? Perhaps you're better off where you are now. The second error you will be committing is that you will be switching everything into last year's winners. And that may mean you are buying close to the top of the market. There is nothing extraordinary about gold doubling and oil tripling (or vice versa). Every year some investments do spectacularly well. If you can guess consistently what these are going to be (and can prove it by your well-kept track record), and if you are willing to risk all your funds on one throw of the dice, then by all means go out and gamble. But if you are not a professional and/or an experienced expert, then set realistic goals for yourself and don't get upset when you hear all those wonderful stories of other people's success. Only a small number of them are true.

Finally, we must repeat the old Wall Street saw: Bulls make money, bears make money, but pigs never do. Never hold out for the last twitch of the price curve. Never hold on to your investments up to the last cent of profit. J.P. Morgan, our famous tycoon of the last epoch, said he had made his money by always selling too soon. On the other hand, don't be too timid. Let your profits run. If you are scared of an imminent collapse of the market, sell *some* of your stocks. This is called averaging, and as we said, it is a good practice if done in moderation. You take some profits but leave some of your money to participate in the bonanza — if indeed it is going to continue.

Against the Madding Crowd: being right before your time

Let's now turn our attention to a question that most investors ask themselves at one time or another: Is it possible for the ordinary individual to beat the odds, start almost from nothing and accumulate a fortune in his lifetime? Most academics and theoreticians would answer in the negative: No one can be a steady winner in the market over a long period of time. In effect, this view holds that no one can be consistently smarter than the majority, and it is based on the idea that whatever the majority do in the market, they are necessarily right, because the market tends to do whatever the majority decide it should do. In practice, however, this view doesn't stand up. The history of the market is riddled with examples of the majority, en masse, doing the wrong thing. In other words, it is possible for the bulk of investors to be shamefully wrong all at the same time. And as a result, it is possible for you to be consistently right over the long term.

How? To answer that question, let's look at the "classical" investment method, also known as the gospel according to Graham and Dodd. These two gentlemen were the grandfathers of the U.S. security analysts, and their investment strategy calls for infrequent and long-term trading. Many veterans of investment wars have been using this strategy, or a derivative of it for years — the two most famous being John Templeton and Warren Buffett. Their success shows that the strategy can work, and it confirms that you can make money by doing what the majority of investors are not doing. John Templeton now lives in the Bahamas, and manages his highly successful Templeton Growth Fund from there. Warren Buffett is a retired investor, at the ripe old age of 46. Both of these gentlemen started with less than $100,000 (most of which was borrowed) and ended up as millionaires several times over.

So what it is Graham and Dodd strategy? Basically, it's a system for investing in "undervalued" securities. Graham and Dodd believed that the market is far from perfect, and that most investors do not know what they are doing. Most of the time, stocks are therefore either overpriced or very much underpriced. The system they developed on this basis is very simple: The individual investor is supposed to scrutinize the market to find good, underpriced stocks, buy them and then hold them for long periods of time. It's as straightforward as that. And although it's easier said than done, it has been successfully applied in practice. Their system is described in their book *Security Analysis*, but we shall list its main points here:

* Buy stocks paying very high dividend yields. Anything above 6% or so will do.
* Look at the balance sheet of the company. It should be reasonably clear of debt. This feature would make the company less prone to bankruptcy in times of recession.
* Look for companies with dominant market positions in their particular line of business.
* Buy the stock only when the price is extremely low. This may be measured by the price-earnings ratio; that is, the ration of the current market price to the expected earnings per share.
* Look for companies that generate a lot of cash.
* Once you buy the stock, hold it, and forget about the level of the market. Ignore short-term fluctuations in price. John Templeton, for instance, holds a stock on average for about four years before he sells it.

Let us now give a clearer picture of what we mean by underpriced stocks. In 1979, the New York market was selling at a collective P/E ratio of about 5 or 6; that is, the average stock price was only 5 or 6 times the average earnings per share. And this, let us remember, was happening at a time when the U.S. dollar was at a record low against most currencies (except for currencies such as the Canadian dollar and the Brazilian cruzeiro). In other words, not only were stocks cheap, but they could also be bought with cheap dollars. In contrast, the New York market in the 1960s sold an average P/E ratio of close to 14. Most observers agree that, even if such heights are not to be reached again, it is not unreasonable to expect a P/E ratio of, say, 10 or 12. If we now assume that corporate profits in the next few years will grow at a rate of 7% or 8% per year — less than the rate of inflation — then by 1984 (in four years' time, which is the period John Templeton recommends for holding a stock), corporate earnings will be about 35% higher than today. If, by that time, the market has reached a collective P/E ratio of 10, then, a stock selling in 1979 for $10 will be selling for $27. That would produce a profit of 28% per year. If the market rose to a level where its P/E ratio was 14, then the same $10 stock would be selling for $38. That would give a profit of 39.6% per annum. It is, therefore, not surprising that both Buffett and Templeton (among others) are very enthusiastic about the long-term prospects of the U.S. market, and about their chances of making money in it.

If you want to follow their lead, then you should adopt some simple rules:

* First, you must closely follow the market, the economy and the world situation.
* You should also start with as high an initial stake as possible. Borrow. The interest is tax-deductible.
* Start as soon as possible and stay as long as possible.
* Don't withdraw any funds from the kitty. Let it grow, and keep reinvesting the dividends.

John Templeton, incidentally, has already spent 40 years at this game. He has seen his fund grow to a value of $240 million. This is a compound growth rate of close to 29% per annum. Warren Buffett started with about the same stake, but he is now worth close to $30 million. The difference is to be found in the method. Buffett started conglomerating when his portfolio became thick enough, and when you start taking over companies, you can make much, much more than 29% per annum. However, before you reach that level you are well advised to stick to the proved Graham and Dodd method. It may be slower. But it is also surer.

Fond Farewells: you only make money when you sell

Almost all the advice you hear on how to make a sound investment is concerned with buy decisions. It points you toward the favored stocks or other investment vehicles that seem likely to increase in value. However, any investment you make, whether successful or not, involves more than just the decision to buy. You also have to sell whatever it is you have bought in order to complete your transaction. In spite of this obvious and elementary fact, very few stock market reports or analysts' recommendations concern themselves with selling. You will probably find, for example, that most of your conversations with your broker focus on what and when to buy, rather than what and when to sell.

It's not too hard to understand why this should be. Investors tend to be optimistic — otherwise they wouldn't be investing — so they concentrate much of their attention on their buy decisions. Then, too, analysts and brokers receive their market information from sources as close as possible to the management of the companies they are following. And company executives like to talk up the positive aspects of their operations and downplay the negatives. Again, this positive talk encourages buy considerations. Also, analysts have a vested interest in supporting the shares of the companies they follow. If their comments were too harsh, they would find themselves less welcome by the company next time they went seeking information, so they are naturally reluctant to antagonize their sources. You can see signs of this bias if you look at the lists of recommendations from any major brokerage house. You will almost always find such lists full of buy and hold recommendations, but noticeably lacking in sell recommendations.

This should not really be the case. After all, every time someone buys, someone else sells — so there are as many sell decisions being made as there are buy decisions. So let's have a look at these sell decisions, and right away remind ourselves of some basic truths. When you buy a stock, it actually costs you money. It is only when you sell the stock that you can possibly make money. Knowing how, what and when to buy is, of course, a necessary prerequisite to showing a profit. But that profit doesn't exist until you sell your holdings and let someone else take up the position you are about to vacate. Selling decisions, in other words, are at least as important as buying decisions. So don't be swayed by the market bias.

Ideally, of course, you should try to sell a stock at a higher price than the one at which you bought it. However, the price at which you buy is relevant only when you buy; as soon as you have bought, the price you paid becomes irrelevant. Most people have difficulty accepting this, because they are always aiming for that ideal of selling at a higher price than the one at which they bought. Nevertheless, once you have bought, the first part of your transaction is complete. It is in the past, and nothing you can do will change it. The only thing that remains now is for you to complete the second part of your transaction—the selling. That means you should only be interested in the present and the future. After you've bought your stock, then, there are really only three questions you should be asking yourself:

* How much could you get if you sold your holdings?
* How much do you think you could get in the future if you maintained your present holdings?

* How much do you think you could get elsewhere if you sold now and put your money into another investment?

As an example, suppose you have bought 100 shares of a company at $15 per share, and the price has now risen to $20 per share. You would probably say that you have made a profit of 33%. But you haven't. You would only make that profit if you sold. So should you sell? Perhaps. It all depends on how you answer the last two questions listed previously. If you think you can earn more by selling your shares now and investing the money elsewhere, then you should sell. If you don't think you can do better elsewhere, then you should hold. It's important, though, to understand our main point here. The fact that you bought the shares at $15 is irrelevant when deciding whether to sell or hold. What you are trying to decide is whether you should sell shares presently valued at $20. If you had bought the shares for $10, $12, $18 or any other price, your dilemma would still be the same: What should you do with your $20 shares — sell or hold? The only thing that should influence your decision is the present and what you expect to see in the future. You should only consider the past in terms of any trend it may indicate — in other words, in terms of what it might tell you about the future.

The same thinking would apply if you had paid $25 for your shares, and seen them drop to $20. Most people in this situation would be inclined to hold on to the shares, hoping they would at least climb back to $25. That way, their original buy decision would be vindicated. However, as we have said, the past is past and cannot change. Once the shares are at $20, they are no longer $25 shares that have fallen in price; they are, quite simply, $20 shares. And your decision on whether to sell or hold is exactly the same as if the shares had risen from $15.

At the risk of repeating ourselves, we will sum up:

* Once you have bought some shares, the only thing you can do with them is hold or sell.
* At all times, you should be asking yourself which option you should select.
* When trying to decide, ignore the past — the price at which you bought — and concentrate only on the present and the future.
* Always ask yourself if you could do better in some other investment, and if the answer is yes, then sell your present holdings — no matter what profit or loss you will show on them — and get into that other, better investment.
* Bear in mind that you only make money when you sell, so give at least as much attention to your sell decisions as you do to your buy decisions.

The Magic of Shorting: selling what you haven't got

Finally, in this section, let's look at a technique that many experienced investors use to increase their profits: selling short — selling into the market securities that you do not own in the hope of being able to buy them later at a lower price. The theory here is quite simple. You will always make money if you buy something at a certain price and sell it later for a higher price. Buy low, sell high — that's the basic market rule.

In a standard stock market transaction, therefore, you buy a stock, hold it until the price goes up; then you sell for a profit. This is called going long. Selling short is just the opposite. You first sell the stock at a certain price, then wait until the price goes down, then you buy the stock. You are still buying at a lower price than the price at which you sell; so you are still making money. The only difference is that you have now reversed the order of your transaction. Most people grasp this easily enough, but they get confused by the question: How can you sell a stock before you've bought it; how can you sell something you don't own? In essence, the answer is that you first borrow the stock.

Let's see how it works in practice, and also see what requirements you have to meet. The requirements we mention here are general ones. There are variances between the Toronto Stock Exchange and the New York Stock Exchange, between the Ontario Securities Commission and the Securities and Exchange Commission, and between one broker and another. Also, the requirements apply to stocks, and are not completely applicable to commodities, options, bonds or currencies. First, you must open a separate "short account" with your broker, and, because borrowing is involved, it must be a "margin account." You must, therefore, sign a "margin agreement," with the appropriate rights, obligations, terms and liabilities included in it.

The most important obligation that you have is to maintain proper margin at all times. Since February 15, 1980, Toronto Stock Exchange margin requirements have been 60%, up from 50%. To go on margin with a 60% margin requirement means that, for every dollar of stock bought long or sold short, you must put up 60 cents in cash, or unencumbered, negotiable and marginable securities with a loan value of 60 cents. To produce a loan value of 60 cents from marginable securities, you must put up $1.50 of such securities, since only 40% of the $1.50 has a loan value (40% x $1.50 = 60 cents). At present, the New York Stock Exchange requires only 50% margin. To be properly margined in a short account, you must have an unencumbered or "free" credit balance equal to 160% of the net proceeds of the sale of the shorted stock.

To illustrate, suppose you sell 100 shares of stock to net $3,000 after commission. Your account must have an additional $1,800 cash in it for a total credit of $4,800. If you do not supply an additional $1,800 in cash, you must provide negotiable, marginable securities with a market value of $4,500 to produce a loan value of $1,800 at 60% margin. Only securities that meet the qualifications and definitions of the relevant regulatory body will be accepted as marginable. Applying the mathematics, you can see that when you go *long* on margin using securities as collateral you require $7,500 of marginable securities with a 40% loan value to carry a $3,000 debit. The debit will cost you 1% above prime interest rate. When you go *short* on margin using securities as collateral, you require only $4,500 of marginable securities with a 40% loan value to carry the additional $1,800 margin required in the short account. The credit does not earn interest. Although your short account is a separate account from your regular long account (which can be cash or margin), securities and margin position shortages are excesses that can be transferred from one account to the other.

Before your short sale can be entered for execution, you must, as we said, arrange to borrow the stock. Although you are selling it short, the buyer on the other side of your sale does not know this. He is making a legitimate purchase and is entitled to the physical delivery of his shares. He pays for this purchase and the credit goes to your account with your broker. If your broker has margin accounts that are long on the stock you are shorting, he can borrow from those positions to deliver the shares to the buyer. You should note that the margin agreement you sign allows your broker to deal with your collateral as he feels is necessary. If you are long on margin, your stock is not usually physically in your account but assigned elsewhere.

When your broker cannot borrow the stock "in-house," he can check the "loan post" of the particular stock you wish to short. If the stock you require is not available either in-house or at the loan post, then you will not be able to make a short sale. No matter how large the number of outstanding shares or float, there may not be stock for loan purposes. At this point your strategy would be defeated.

But let's assume you can borrow the stock at the loan post. The lender usually requires a premium above the market for the use of his stock. That is, if the market value is, say, $3,000, you may have to provide $3,100 as collateral for the borrowed stock. Also, if dividends are paid when you are short, the lender of the stock is entitled to them, as is the purchaser. In effect, you will receive one dividend but pay two. And this, of course, will have an impact on the cost of the short sale.

Now that you have arranged to borrow the stock, you can proceed with the short sale. (This borrowing process may have taken a couple of days and your timing could now be too late.) Your salesman enters your order as a short sale, and the floor trader is advised of this. On the TSE, a short sale can only be made on an "up-tick," which means that it must be made at a price above the last board-lot sale. The theory is that this rule prevents short sales from driving down the market, and becoming self-fulfilling. This makes it difficult to sell short when the market is very quiet or in a down trend, so it is a subtle way of discouraging short selling. The NYSE requires that the short be made at the "last-tick," which is a little easier to execute. Your broker and his floor trader know of all registered short sales, and they are required to report them to the exchanges. The buyer's broker does not know, although he may suspect, that the stock has now been shorted.

As long as the lender of the stock does not call your loan and your account is properly margined, you can wait for the price to decline. You receive no interest on the credit balance and, as long as no dividends are payable, you are only out of interest on your margin. When the stock reaches your downside objective, you "buy in," return the borrowed stock, receive the collateral back, and put the profit in your pocket. However, the lender of the stock may decide he wants his stock back. If this happens and you cannot replace the borrowed stock, you are *forced* to buy in. This could be at an adverse time in the market, and could cost you dearly if the stock has moved up. When you buy on margin, you know that zero is the lowest price you can receive for your long position. But when you sell short, you could pay anything for the stock to replace it.

Short selling is a negative approach to the market, and, because security trading is traditionally based on buying or going long, you are in opposition to the market. Sometimes, of course, this can be the most profitable approach to take. Always remember, though, that the risk can be high if your borrowed stock is called at an awkward time or if your assessment of the market is totally wrong. It is only appropriate for those with determination and strong stomachs. If you decide to try it at all, it's best to short slowly and cautiously. That could mean shorting a mutual fund or even a market fund (a so-called index fund). In the former case, you're shorting a collection of stocks — as many as are held by the fund — not just one stock. In the latter case, you're shorting the entire market. And that can be a worthwhile move — if you're sure that the total market is due for a fall.

More On Risk: sexy blondes versus good plain cooks

All of us at one time or another have searched for that unusual opportunity that will allow us to earn a much-better-than-average return on investment. Long-range planning and slow steady growth is the assured route to financial security and therefore the best one to follow, but at the same time, there's no point in denying that most of us would still like to make a fast dollar. So let's look now at some ways of beating the odds to increase your return.

Right away, the problem here is that, as a general rule, any attempt to raise your return also raises your risk. You may aim for that increased return, but in the process you may just end up with an unpleasant loss. But is there a way of raising your return without also increasing your risk? Basically, the answer is yes — if you can find a good opportunity and take advantage of it before it has had time to pass. That answer may seem a little unsatisfactory, but if we look at some specifics, we may see how it can be put into practice.

In the first of our discussions on this topic, let's look at the way you can spot a stock market opportunity that can be in the making if a large, well-established company runs into temporary difficulties. The short-term problems will likely depress the company's share prices, giving you a chance to buy in at a low level, and if the company is still basically sound, its share price will one day bounce back, and you will have made yourself a reasonable profit. So there is an opportunity here. But what is the best way to take advantage of it? Essentially, you have to realize that any major development that affects a company's fortunes, someone likely will win and someone likely will lose. The trick, then, is to be on the side of the winners, and the best way to do that is to tie your fortunes in with the group that has the most clout to control the final outcome — the group that is most likely to emerge on the side of the winners.

We will elaborate on that. But first, let's take a look at the nature of corporate obligations to see whose interests are most likely to be best looked after. Corporate obligations — the obligations that companies have toward investors — come in various forms, but basically there are only two main types: debt obligations and ownership obligations. Debt obligations take the form of bonds; that is, the company issuing the bonds is obliged to pay interest to the bond holders at a predetermined rate and at predetermined times. It must also return the money it borrowed, either in one lump sum at the end of a specified period (known as a balloon payment), or in gradual installments that will bring the outstanding amount to zero at the end of the period (known as a "sinking" fund). Ownership obligations, on the other hand, come in the form of shares. They carry no obligations similar to those associated with bonds; instead they are just testimonials that you own a piece of the company.

Our main point here, however, is that these obligations are ranked in order of priority. Bonds impose a greater obligation on companies than do stocks, of course. But within the two groups, there is a further distinction of rank: Some bonds rank higher than other bonds, and some shares rank higher than other shares (preferreds over common, for example). Suppose then, that an established company gets into difficulty. What happens to its various obligations? First to go will be the payment of dividends to common shareholders. The company has no contractual obligations to pay dividends on its common stock, so these dividends can be suspended without putting the company into default. Next to go would be dividends on the preferred shares. Again, there is no contractual obligation to maintain them. However, the dividends are cumulative and would eventually have to be paid. And no dividends could be paid on the common shares until all the arrears on the preferreds had been paid. Last to go would be the interest payments on debt obligations, which would put the company into technical default. A company in this situation is in serious difficulty and is unlikely to represent an opportunity. Its problems are probably too deeply ingrained, so it should be avoided.

Suppose, though, that you find a company that is in difficulty only to the extent that it has dropped its dividend payments on its common and preferred shares. If the company's fortunes seem likely to improve, then this could be an opportunity for you to make a profitable investment. And, as we indicated, the best way to profit is to hitch your fortunes to the group that seems most likely to determine future events. Such a group, in most cases, would be the group that holds the control block of common shares.

Let's see how it would work, using Massey-Ferguson as a specific example. As you may realize, Massey-Ferguson recently ran into financial difficulties that caused it to drop its dividends on both its common and preferred shares, although the dividends on the preferreds were, and are, cumulative. The company also has a control block of shares that are held by Argus Corp. The only real way that Argus could profit from its investment was if the dividends on the common shares were reinstated. However, dividends on the common could not be reinstated until the arrears on the preferreds were fully paid off because of the hierarchy of corporate obligations. Therefore, it was in Argus' interest to see that the dividends on the preferreds were paid in full and as quickly as possible. Here then, is the setting for the opportunity. And since Argus was the holder of the control block, it was the group to side with.

This is how the opportunity developed: Massey-Ferguson has two types of preferred shares, A and B, both having a par value of $25 per share, yielding 10% at par or a dividend of $2.50 per share. In the past, the shares had traded as high as $27½ and as low as $17⅝. At the time, they were trading at $19⅜. Clearly, the thing to do was buy the preferreds at that price, since then you would be aligning yourself with the interests of the controlling shareholder. Once Massey-Ferguson recovered its financial footing — as presumably it would, since it wasn't about to go out of business — the preferred dividends would be reinstated (as Argus wanted) and the arrears would be paid off. At that point, the preferred shareholders stood to make a sizable killing.

This, in fact, is exactly what happened. Massey-Ferguson announced a major refinancing program, which (to no one's surprise) included the reinstatement of those $2.50 dividends and the payoff of the accumulated arrears. And on the day of the announcement, the preferreds jumped sharply in price. On that day, the A preferreds closed at $25.12, and the B preferreds closed at $24.87. Meanwhile, on the downside, there had never been any real risk involved in buying the preferreds. It's true that the preferreds could have slipped a little in price. But remember that those unpaid dividends on the preferreds were cumulative. Sooner or later they would be paid, and anyone who believed that Massey-Ferguson was going to stay in business was aware that they'd be paid. Therefore, there was a floor price below which the preferreds were unlikely to fall. This, then, is the kind of situation you should keep a lookout for. It gives you that opportunity to earn a higher-than-average return. But it doesn't mean that you necessarily have to accept an increased risk.

Spotting Sleepers: big guys in little companies

Next to fishermen, investors are the one group of people most likely to break your heart with a tale about the one that got away. All of us, at one time or another, have failed to act when we should have done so, and have been forced to sit back and watch as our missed opportunity proved highly profitable — for someone else. In the context, we may safely say that it is the fondest wish of every investor to chance upon a budding Xerox or IT&T, at a time when it is still in its infancy and can be purchased for little more than a song. As it happens, skilled investors, like hawk-eyed baseball scouts, can identify future stars while they are still young. And, invariably, one of the most important qualities they look for is good, solid management.

It is a common fallacy that the key factor in a company's success is its product. Xerox, according to this belief, could not have failed to succeed. Its product was so much in demand, and protected by patents, too, that no matter what the company did, it was bound to turn into a success. This is not necessarily the case. We have all seen companies, even in growth industries, go belly-up for a number of reasons, none of which is connected with the companies' products. This could have happened to Xerox had it not had what all successful companies have: the right people in the right places doing the correct things at the proper time. Management, in other words, is the one factor that most separates a "me-too" company from a genuine shooting star.

As an example, let's look at the beer market in the U.S. For a long time, the market was dominated by five large national firms. But then a tough newcomer, Philip Morris, bought up one of the firms, Miller, and began chasing a larger share of the pie. From that point on, Miller became something of a star performer, boosting its worth by many millions of dollars, and forcing the other breweries to react to its initiative. The company and its product were essentially unchanged; the sudden strength came almost entirely from the new management and its aggressive growth-oriented stance. As a result, it is certainly worthwhile looking at the people who run the company in which you're thinking of investing. They can be a good indication of whether or not you'll be able to boost your return on investment to above-average levels.

Now, as we all know, there are a lot of companies around that are top-heavy with distinguished-looking executives, who not only look like managers, but talk like managers and play golf too. Many of them, however, simply do not know how to manage successfully. Management is getting results. Those who get results are good managers. Those who don't, aren't. It really is that simple. No one knows this better than the venture capitalists who gamble millions on the talent of one or several managers, taking a chance on a new company that hasn't yet proved its worth. This is how Pop Shoppes was started. Amdahl, too — the new rival of IBM — was started this way; and so too was De Lorean Motor Car Co., the new sports car company that was launched by a former General Motors executive. For our purposes, then, we should be looking for young companies that fulfill two conditions: First, they must be publicly traded, preferably at a low price; and second, they must be well managed with a definite emphasis being placed on growth.

So how do we find them? Let's look first at a company that has already proved itself successful: Dome Petroleum. Dome Petroleum is a giant today, but it hasn't always been that way. Only a few years ago its shares were trading at less than a quarter of the price they now fetch. Dome's success came about because it assembled one of the best management teams in the oil industry, and then it oriented itself toward growth by taking calculated risks right and left. One of the points that some investors always found appealing was the absolute trust the managers of the company had in their own abilities. This trust was underlined by the fact that they put all their pension funds into Dome's own stock. From the point of view of prudence and caution, this might seem to have been folly. But from the point of view of shareholders, it was by itself a guarantee that management in this company would not be sleeping on the job. Even today, when Dome's management could possibly rest on its past successes, the company is still growing and still taking risks; it is among the many companies now searching for oil and gas in the Arctic.

It is, of course, not possible (or even particularly desirable) to follow the pension schemes of the companies whose stocks you are thinking of buying. But one thing you can watch for is the progress of key management people who have well-proved management skills. It is, for example, becoming quite common for the top managers of large corporations to join, or even launch, small companies of their own, which they can manage specifically for growth. If you find, or read about, one of these companies, it is certainly worth keeping an eye on. The people behind it have the skills to run the company effectively, and they have the track record necessary to raise the financial backing.

A common strategy for management stars is to purchase a publicly traded company — preferably on a tranquil stock exchange such as Vancouver, and preferably one that is riddled with tax losses. The company that is purchased is really little more than a corporate shell, which is then capitalized — injected with cash or other assets — and used to purchase other, more profitable, companies. This is one way in which conglommerates are born. The advantage of the tax losses is seen when the budding conglomerate begins to make money; the tax losses can then be used to offset taxes on the new profits. Since all this activity is taking place within the framework of a publicly traded company, you are able to piggyback on the company's success by buying its shares.

So, for each small company whose shares you are tempted to buy, you should first check the background and other current activities of its principal managers and directors. Initially, your best source for this kind of information is The Financial Post's *Directory of Directors*. But after a while, you will become familiar with a surprisingly large number of big corporate names and you will then be able to follow their careers with relative ease and considerable interest. And if you should find a small, publicly traded company whose leaders seem to be disproportionately famous, skilled or experienced, then you may be fairly confident that its shares are potential above-average winners. All this, of course, does not mean that you should ignore the appropriate analysis of the numbers surrounding the company and its performance; it is, instead, a reminder that it is the management of the company that is responsible for creating those numbers in the first place.

Watching the Insiders: sexy blondes who can also cook

In an earlier discussion, we said that there are two main ways to make money in the stock market. The first calls for careful analysis of corporate reports and financial statements, intense research and patient forecasting. The second calls for inside information. The first method should get you an annual return of 15%-20% per year. The second method may double your money in a year — but put you in jail in two. Fortunately, though, there is a way to combine the attractions of the second method with the safety of the first. And that is to watch the people who have inside information — the corporate insiders — and then do as they do.

Corporate insiders, contrary to many people's belief, can and do invest in shares of their own companies. After all, they are in the game for the money. (Power is nice, yes, but you can't put it into your bank account.) Naturally, there are things that insiders cannot do without committing a crime. They cannot, for example, buy and sell for a quick profit. So it is not kosher for the president of Gulf Canada, say, to buy Gulf shares with the knowledge of an Hibernia strike and then sell them a week later. However, it is acceptable if he (and all other insiders in Gulf) buys shares of Gulf — and then holds them. In other words, stock market regulators allow proper insider trading, but attempt to plug the improper profiteering. The easiest way to do this is to force all insiders to file a report of their trading in their company's shares with the security commission of the exchange where those shares are traded.

Obviously, it can be very instructive to watch the

moves made by these corporate leaders. You can bet that they have a good idea of what's going to happen to their companies. You can also bet that they are going to act in their own self-interest. As a result, they can often give you some useful clues on which way they think the market for a particular stock is going to move. So how can you find out what the insiders are doing? One way is to read those reports of insider trading. The Ontario Securities Commission, for example, puts out such a report once a month, and it is fascinating reading for anyone with his money riding in the market. It can be obtained directly from the OSC, or — even better — its more salient points can be found, once a month, in *The Globe and Mail*'s *Report on Business* section. We suggest you look for it.

Of course, when the report is published in the newspaper, the action it describes is already a month or two old. There is a month from the actual transaction until the date of filing (the insider has about 30 days to tell of his trades); a few weeks for the report itself to be published; and the *Globe* takes a day or two, as well, to sift through the facts and print them. Nevertheless, the information is still relevant. For one thing, most insiders are with the corporation to stay. Also, as we said, frequent trading in the shares of their company is frowned upon by the law, so purchases of shares by corporate insiders are generally long-term investments.

There are several rules to keep in mind when reading the report of insiders' trading. First, remember that not all the trades are significant. Some are minor, and some have motives behind them that have no relationship to yours. Second, always look at what the most important people in the company are doing. Is the chairman buying or selling? What are the directors doing? These are the insiders most in the know. Vice-presidents, say, normally see only a corner of the picture (unless they are also on the board). Third, watch out for one company buying another. Sometimes it is a good sign. If the first company thinks the second company is a good investment, perhaps it knows something you don't. But it is also possible that the first company wants to get 51% (control) of the second company, so it can milk it through intercompany sales, loans, salaries to directors, and so on. Fourth, watch out for "washout sales." Some directors and officers hold shares in their companies through personal holding companies. When such a company is created, you will see the sale by the insider of the shares "beneficially owned," and the purchase by the insider's personal holding company. This means nothing to you, since no net sale or purchase has taken place. Fifth, look for the absolute level of holdings of the insider. If it is high, the insider has a heavy stake in the shares, and therefore will try to see to it that they rise in price. The higher the stake, the higher the incentive. You, of course, can tag along on his coattails.

Let's now look at an actual insiders' trading report; a fairly typical one, taken from a recent edition of *The Globe and Mail.* The first item in this particular report shows that Montagu and Conrad Black are consolidating their empire. The Blacks, you may remember, control Hollinger Mines (now Hollinger Argus), Dominion Stores, Massey-Ferguson and other companies through Ravelston Corp. Well, the insider report shows that the Blacks have just bought some more of what they already have — the report says that Ravelston, which the Blacks control, has bought 100,000 more shares of Hollinger Argus. This indicates that the Blacks think that the future of their empire is sound. And as a corroborating piece of data, Argus Corp. also bought about 95,000 more shares of Dominion Stores.

A second item in the report shows that Nathan Starr, a director and the chief executive officer of Acklands, has bought about 19,000 shares, and now holds 420,000. Acklands was in quite a bit of trouble a few years back, and Starr and his colleagues attempted a rescue operation. Nothing drastic — just a few cost-cutting measures, tightening operations, and so on. Now Starr has bought some more shares. But not very many, compared with the number he already owns. This is a statement of confidence in the future of the company — but it's not a particularly strong one. It calls only for cautious optimism re the future of the shares (to use broker's parlance).

Let's skip a few minor items, and we see that Pagurian Press has just bought a few more shares of Black Photo Corp. Pagurian used to be a subsidiary of Interpublishing (an ex-VSE company). It tendered for the shares of its corporate parent in a neat manoeuvre, got some financing from a British peer, and is now creeping up stealthily on Black Photo. If it thinks Black Photo is a good investment, perhaps you should too. Further down the list, we see that Sam Pollock, a Bronfman associate (and now also a director of Brascan) has bought 5,000 Brascan shares, to hold 7,550. This is a purchase worth more than $100,000. Does Sam Pollock know something we don't know? Is Brascan planning something? Is it going to throw itself on Labatt? Or Noranda? Perhaps it's worth investigating.

Even further down the list of insider trading, we can see that a director of Canadian Tire has *sold* 50,000 shares, to hold 121,000 shares. Now this is only one director. If one director is buying, it is a good signal for you to look into the company. But if only one director sells, this can mean almost anything — a son getting married, a daughter going to college, the director himself retiring or planning to buy a house, and so on. People sell for a variety of reasons. It is only when a few directors and insiders sell together that it is really significant.

To repeat: Even when only one insider buys a large number of shares, it usually means he thinks his company has a bright future. We should qualify that, however: The insider must buy his shares on the outside market. If the shares are bought from the company itself ("treasury shares"), this could represent a cash injection by a dominant shareholder — and this would be a sign of trouble. Finally, the great thing about watching insider trading is that you are seeing what people do with their own money. You're not just listening to what people are telling you you should be doing with yours.

When the Elephants Mate: spotting takeovers in advance

One of the most satisfying investments you can make is to buy the shares of a company and then watch those shares jump in price by 20% or even 30% soon after you buy them. Unfortunately, such successes are rare. Also, it seems that all too often they come about largely as the result of luck. However, as we are trying to establish in this section of our book, it is possible to identify those companies whose shares may be in for a dramatic increase in price — or to put it another way, it's possible to increase your chances of making a quick market killing.

One of the best ways of doing this — and the one we'll examine here — is to buy the shares of potential takeover candidates; that is, to identify those companies that seem likely to be taken over by other companies, and then buy their shares before a takeover bid is made. If a takeover bid is then made, you will enjoy that quick market killing, because the price offered for shares in a takeover is almost always substantially higher than the prevailing market price. As a general rule, in fact, the takeover bid will be made at a price that is as much as 20% above the market price. And you, as a holder of shares in the taken-over company, will suddenly be that much richer.

Let's break this subject down and examine it in some detail, looking first at the reason a company would pay such a high premium for the shares of another company. When you, as an individual, buy the shares of a company, the chances are you do not want to exert any real control over the management of that company. All you want to do is be able to sell your shares at some point in the future to someone else — someone who is willing to pay more for the shares than you did. This is fortunate, since the number of shares that you typically buy is going to be so small compared with the total number of outstanding shares, that you couldn't exert any real control, even if you wanted to.

When a corporation buys shares of another company, however, its motivation is somewhat different from yours. It likely will not be looking for a quick capital gain; instead, it will really want to gain control. There are several reasons why a corporation would want to buy control of another. For example, an acquiring company may decide it is simply cheaper to buy another company and its production facilities, than it is to build new production facilities on its own, starting from scratch. Or, an acquiring company may decide that the only way to gain control of a valuable asset is to buy a company that already owns that asset — for example, an oil company that owns large tracts of unexplored land, or a cable television company that has a local monopoly. Also, an acquiring company may benefit from a tax point of view if it takes over another company. For example, if the takeover candidate has a "tax-loss carry-forward," — if it has past losses that can be used to offset future tax liabilities — then the acquiring company may be able to use that tax-loss carry-forward to reduce its own liabilities. Finally, an acquiring company may want to gain control of another company in order to improve its own cash flow. The takeover candidate may, for example, have plenty of cash on hand, and the acquiring company may want to get its hands on that cash once it has gained control, which it can do simply by increasing dividend payments.

Whatever the reason, though, the acquiring company will want to gain control of the takeover candidate, not just acquire a small part of it. In Canada, a company can have complete control of another if it owns more than 50% of the second company's shares. In that situation, it will be able to elect all of the second company's directors. It is not, therefore, necessary for a company to acquire 100% of the company. Equally, though, an acquiring company can sometimes wield effective control if it has less than 50% of the second company's shares. This brings us back to the reason a company will pay a premium for the shares of another company. It doesn't just want a few shares to hold for capital gain; it wants a large number of shares, sufficient to give it the control it is seeking. And only by offering a premium can it be sure that a sufficient number of shares, to give it that control, will be tendered in response to its offer.

So how, then, do you spot potential takeover candidates? First, the potential candidate must be able to offer other companies a *reason* for taking it over. Secondly, it should be able to offer an acquiring company a *means* of taking it over. Let's look at the reasons for a takeover. We have suggested some possible ones above, but there is one other important one: if a company has a book value that is higher than its stock market value. The book value of a company is basically the sum of its assets minus its liabilities, as we explained earlier. If this value is higher than the stock market value — the price at which the company can be acquired through the purchase of shares — then clearly the company is a prime takeover candidate. An acquiring company would be able to buy more than it paid for.

As for the method of a takeover, most acquiring companies like, ideally, to be able to engineer a takeover at no cost to themselves. In other words, they like to use the takeover candidate's money to pay for the cost of the takeover. For example, suppose an acquiring company decides to borrow the funds it needs to complete a takeover, and suppose it can borrow at an interest rate of 12%. Since the marginal corporate tax rate in Canada is approximately 50%, and since interest costs are a tax-deductible business expense, the real cost of the funds to the acquiring corporation would be about 6%, not 12%. Suppose now that the takeover candidate has a dividend yield of about 6%. Once the acquiring corporation has completed its first takeover, it would receive that 6% yield on its invested funds. And this income could then be used to pay the interest on the borrowed funds. In other words, any company that has a dividend yield of approximately 6% is a possible self-financing acquisition. And any company with a dividend substantially higher than 6% could be a very attractive takeover candidate.

Two other factors should also be considered when looking for takeover candidates. First, if a company is particularly large, with a high number of expensive shares, it will be difficult for another company to acquire a controlling interest. It would cost too much money. As a result, you will find most of your potential takeover candidates among the small- and medium-sized firms. Second, if a company has a large outstanding block of shares that can be purchased by an acquiring company, it may be a potential takeover candidate, but it will *not* be one that is of any value to you. The acquiring company may simply buy the outstanding block and bypass you altogether. The only way you benefit in a takeover is if someone buys the shares you own. Only then will you get the premium price that you are after. To sum up: Any time there exists a possibility for a corporate acquisitor to benefit by buying control of another company, there exists the possibility of profit for you — if you take a plunge and buy the shares of the takeover candidate before a bid is made.

Let's suppose now that you have analyzed the balance sheet of a company — Company X — and you've decided a takeover is likely, so you've bought 100 Company X common shares. Book value of the company is, say, $20 per share, while the market price, reflecting the quality of management, is just $10 per share. You hold the stock for several months, until one day Company Y comes out of the woodwork and bids $12.50 per share. You congratulate yourself for your wisdom, but then you think, should you tender your shares? The answer is not always obvious, because the bid for your Company X can be made in several different ways:

1. The offer may be for all the shares of Company X.
2. The offer may be for part of the shares (normally 51%).
3. The payment may be in cash.
4. The payment may be in shares of the acquiror, Company Y.
5. The payment may be made in debentures (bonds).
6. The payment may be made in any combination of the above.

It begins to get complicated. Let us say that Company Y tenders for only 51% of the outstanding common shares of Company X, and it offers hard cash. What should you do? First of all you should remember that, in Canada, 51% of the votes entitles the holder to nominate the entire board of directors, and the 49% minority has no say at all in future corporate affairs, such as dividends. If you tender your 100 shares, the chances are that only 51 of them will be taken up by the purchaser, since he is obligated to buy the tendered shares "pro rata." This is so for obvious reasons: no preferential treatment for large blocks. So, you would receive $12.50 x 51 = $637.50 for 51 of your 100 shares. Now you turn around and sell the other 49 shares — for how much?

That's a very good question. What *is* the share price post-acquisition? Remember, the new owner will have control of the company, its cash and its business, and he may use this control to benefit *his* business (Company Y). For instance, he may sell to Company X some less-than-sterling-quality assets held by Company Y. In that way, he transfers the cash of Company X to his control at Company Y. It is, therefore, entirely possible that the price of the shares *not* taken up by the acquiror will drop even lower than the original price of $10. If it drops below $7.50 (disregarding commissions for a moment), you may even lose from a takeover bid that should make you money. So, should you tender your shares at a partial bid? The answer is not simple. You should decide by regarding the acquiring company as a business you are being asked to buy. After all, it will be managing your 49 remaining shares. Do you want it to do this? If you do, then tender. If not, then don't.

Let's look at another situation where you are offered "paper" for your shares. Here, the acquiror proposes that you give him your shares of Company X in exchange for his shares (either common or preferred) or his debentures (bonds). As before, you have to remember that the only factor you should consider is the sale value of the package *after* the tender offer is completed.

Let's complicate matters a little further. Using the previous example, let us suppose that Company Y's takeover attempt is vehemently resisted by Company X. Suppose, too, that Company Z, with the open support of Company X's management, then makes a competing bid. This new bid is also at $12.50, but it is for 100% of the shares. You, of course, would choose the second bid, as it enables you to take your money and run. However, out comes Company Y with a counter-counter-bid — a combination of securities and cash. Suppose it bids $5 in cash, a preferred share with a face value of $5 and a coupon rate of 8%, and a bond with a face value of $5 and an interest rate of 9%. This adds up to $15 compared with $12.50.

Now, how do you decide what to do? Let us start by stating that the value of each security is only what you can sell it for. Thus, a preferred share with a face value (also called "par value") of $5 will actually sell for $5 *only* if the coupon rate is equal to the yield the market of the day required for an equivalent risk. The same may be said for a bond. If, for instance, the rate of interest is deemed to be too low for a risk such as the combined corporation represents, then the bond will be traded at a discount. This is a factor you should certainly consider, because only then will you be able to tell which offer is really better.

Another factor to consider is that, often, many shares change hands *after* the tender offer is announced. When there is still some uncertainty as to the outcome of the offer, the shares will trade at a slight discount from the offer price. They will then be picked up by "arbitrageurs," who, for the sake of a quick profit, are willing to undertake the extra risk of the deal not going through. Such arbitrageurs operate with very short-term funds (called "overnight money") borrowed from a generous banker for that specific purpose. You can rest assured that any package of securities that they receive will be promptly sold to repay the loans, once the deal has, in fact, gone through. Their shares and bonds therefore, create an enormous "overhang" on the market, which, when sold, will act to depress the price. As a result, you may find that the value of your "package" of Company Y securities is worth less than you originally thought.

Finally, since we live in an imperfect world, let us not neglect the question of tax. When you tender your Company X shares for cash, you have to pay tax, as you have sold them at a profit. There are some cases when the payment of cash can be thinly disguised as a "deem" dividend. In such cases, you may even save some tax if Revenue Canada will accept your arguments. We'll discuss this in our section on taxes. In contrast, the exchange of a security for another security is generally a case of "barter" — and therefore tax-free. As a result, an exchange of shares, objectively valued at, say, $13 each, may at times be worth more to you than a cash offer of $14 per share.

As you can see, takeovers offer several opportunities for profit. But choosing a potential takeover candidate is only half the story. You also have to learn how to evaluate the different bids that may be made, to decide which is the best one for you. The rule of thumb, as we mentioned, is the value of the "package" *after* the tender offer has been made and the deal has gone through. In the case of a 100% cash offer, the decision is straightforward. In cases of competing bids, or when you are offered a "package of securities," the realizable cash price of the "package" is the key factor to consider.

Reinvestment Plans: a juicy wave of the future

In recent years, a number of companies have offered their shareholders the chance to reinvest their dividends in the purchase of additional shares of the company, rather than taking the dividends in the form of cash. Usually, the terms under which the additional shares may be purchased are much more attractive than the terms under which you would normally buy the shares on the open market. For this reason, those shares can lead to some extra profit for you — without any additional risk.

As an example, let's have a look at the reinvestment plan that Bell Canada introduced a couple of years ago. Briefly, the main features of this plan are:

1. As a shareholder, you can use your dividends to buy additional shares directly from the company, without paying any fees or commissions of any kind.
2. You will also be able to use your dividends to buy additional shares at a price that is 5% lower than a defined average market price.

Right away you benefit in two ways. In addition, the Bell Canada plan — like other, similar plans — offers the advantages of compounding. This also allows you to earn a higher return. Let's see how it works.

At the time the plan was introduced, Bell Canada shares paid a dividend of $4.20 per share per year. This dividend was distributed in four quarterly installments of $1.05 each, payable on January 15, April 15, July 15, and October 15. Suppose you had purchased 100 shares of Bell Canada early in the year for a total cost, including brokerage, of $5,500, which is what 100 Bell Canada shares would have cost soon after the company introduced its reinvestment plan. On April 15, you would have received your first dividend of $1.05 per share, or, with 100 shares to your name, a total of $105. That money, as we said, could be used to purchase additional Bell Canada shares at a price that is 5% below a defined average market price. In this case, the defined average market price is the average market price taken over the five trading days preceding the April 15 dividend payment.

Let's say that the average market price for Bell Canada shares over that five-day period was $55.78 per share (this was before the shares were split three for one). You would have been entitled to buy new shares at 95% of that price; that is, at 0.95 x $55.78 = $52.99 per share. You would have paid no commission or fees, so your $105 of dividends would all have been used to buy shares, and at $52.99 per share, your $105 would have bought $105 ÷ $52.99 = 1.9815 new shares. Your total holdings then would have been 101.9815 shares.

On July 15, the next date on which dividends were paid, you would, of course, have been entitled to dividends on your additional shares too, so that you would have received $1.05 x 101.9815 = $107.08. The average price of Bell Canada shares during the five days of trading preceding July 15 was, let's say, $57.28. Investing $107.08 in new shares at a price that is 95% of that $57.28 would have allowed you to purchase 1.9677 new shares:

$$\frac{\$107.08}{0.95 \times \$57.28} = 1.9677$$

As a result, by reinvesting your dividends, you would have received a total of 1.9815 + 1.9677 = 3.9492 new shares in the six months since the beginning of the year when you purchased your original shares. Since Bell Canada shares then moved up to $59, your 3.9492 new shares would have been worth $232.99. And since your original investment was $5,500, this would have given you an annualized yield of 8.47%. In contrast, had you taken your dividends as cash and not compounded them by reinvestment, you would have received $210. On your $5,500 initial investment, this would have given you an annualized yield of 7.64% — considerably lower.

Two other points are worth mentioning here. First, if you sell the shares you bought at 95% of the market price — the shares you purchased with your dividends — you would not trigger a capital gain of 5% on each. Instead, the capital gain you would trigger would be calculated on the basis of the average price you paid for *all* your shares. This average would, of course, be higher than 95% of the market price. This would, therefore, have the effect of reducing your capital gain on the shares you bought with your reinvested dividends, which, in turn, means that the capital gains tax you would have to pay on these shares would also be reduced. Second, although you are reinvesting your dividends in new shares, your dividends are still eligible for the dividend tax credit.

Of course, underlying all the benefits of dividend reinvestment plans is the fact that you must still like the stock you are buying for its own sake. Don't be lured into a stock only because it offers a reinvestment plan. View the reinvestment plan as a profitable way in which you can build your holdings in a stock that you already like. Reinvestment plans are still relatively new to Canada. However, apart from Bell Canada, these other companies offer such plans: British Columbia Telephone, Calgary Power, Canada Development Corp., Canadian Pacific, Interprovincial Pipe Line Ltd., Iron Bay Trust, National Trust, Union Gas Ltd., Victoria and Grey Trust, and most mutual funds. Other companies will soon be introducing plans too. So keep an eye out for them, and see if you think it is worth your while to use one to build your holdings in a stock that especially appeals to you.

Lovely Leverage: warrants and call options

One of the best ways of raising the return on your invested capital is to use leverage. And in the stock market, the best way to do that is to buy warrants and/or call options, instead of the actual stocks themselves. Warrants and call options allow you to participate fully in the movement of the share prices, but they require a much smaller outlay of funds than does the purchase of the shares. Also, they can give you a greater return on your capital. To put that another way, their upside potential is greater, but so is their downside potential. However, because only a small investment is required, the size of your maximum potential loss is small.

Let's look at warrants first. When interest rates are high, companies find it expensive to raise money by issuing standard bonds or debentures. One way they get around this problem is to attach "stock purchase warrants" to their bonds and debentures. These warrants cost the company nothing to issue, but they make the debt instrument attractive, and so they can reduce the company's borrowing rate. As an added advantage, they can produce additional equity capital for the company at some point in the future, again at no cost to the company. Each warrant will have an "exercise" price, which is the price at which the warrant holder can buy a share of the issuing company. The exercise price is often higher than the current market price of the shares, and it has a certain, finite lifetime.

As an example, Jannock Ltd. issued warrants in July, 1977 to purchase Class A Jannock shares at $12 each until July 31, 1982, and then at $15 per share until July 31, 1987. The market price of the Jannock shares at that time was about $9. The warrants could have been bought for $1.75. This, of course, is one immediate advantage of buying warrants: They are cheap. To buy 100 Jannock warrants at that time would have cost you less than $200. To buy 100 Jannock shares, you would have had to spend close to $1,000. The second advantage is to be found in the return on investment. About a year or so after the warrants were issued, Jannock shares were trading at around $20, an increase of 122%.

But as the share price moved up, so, too, did the price of the warrants. They rose to $11.50 per share, an increase of 576%. As a rule, as the share price moves up, the warrant price moves up, too, dollar for dollar. If the Jannock shares had then gone from $20 to $30, an increase of 50%, then the warrants would have gone from $11.50 to $21.50, an increase of 87%. If the price of the Jannock shares had declined, however, the price of the warrants would also have declined, again on a dollar-for-dollar basis. Your percentage loss would then have been greater with the warrants than it would have been with the shares. Remember, though, that with the warrants you only have to invest a relatively small amount of money, so the maximum loss you can suffer is considerably smaller too.

Now, let's look at call options. Similar in many ways to warrants, they are still relatively new in Canada. Basically, a call option gives you the right to buy a set number of shares of a specific stock at a fixed, or "strike," price, within a fixed and specified period of time. Suppose, for example, that you have your eye on Stelco shares, which we'll say are trading at $29 per share. If you were to buy 100 of these shares, it would cost you

$2,900 plus brokerage of $49, for a total of $2,949. Suppose the shares then increased in price within six months, to, say $35 per share. If you sold, you would then realize a gain of 18.7%.

However, until recently it was possible to buy a single call option contract that allowed you to buy 100 shares of Stelco at $30 per share for a specified period of time. That contract would have cost you $200 (or $2 per share), plus brokerage of $15, for a total of $215. If, within the six months, Stelco shares had traded up to that $35, then your call option contract would have been worth at least $5 per share ($35-$30), or $500. Your gain would then have been nearly $300 on an investment of $215, which is a return of 140% — considerably better than the 18.7% return you would have received from the shares. Again, if the price of Stelco stock had declined, your maximum loss would have been restricted to the amount you invested, which in our example was just $215. If you had bought the shares and they had declined in price, you could easily have lost more than this.

Warrants and options, then, are convenient investment vehicles that allow you to participate in the stock market without making a large investment, but with the chance of a high return, and a limited potential loss.

Discount Brokers: how to slash commissions

Most of the recommendations you get from your broker merely tell you what stock is considered "desirable." The price at which you might be able to buy that stock is usually quoted. But most likely, there will be no mention of the equally important price at which you might be able to sell. Also, it almost goes without saying that there will be no mention of commissions. Why should this be? Why is your broker so keen to avoid mentioning commissions? One reason might be that commissions are variable. They depend on the amount you invest, the number of shares you buy, and the price you pay for those shares. But another reason might be that, if you were to dwell too long on commissions, you might never make a stock investment at all, since commission rates in Canada are set by a cartel, and, as a result, they are extremely high. It is quite easy for you to lose 5% of the value of your capital merely by selling a stock at the price at which you bought it. This 5% is not a trivial amount, especially when you consider that most investors expect to earn about 15%-20% on their money, if they are lucky. So let's have a look at these commissions, and some ways to reduce them, so that your return will be increased.

According to the rules published by the Canadian stock exchanges, the base commission rates are as follows:

Share price	*Commission*
$0.005-$5.00	3% of transaction value
$5.00-$15.00	2% of transaction value plus 5¢ per share
$15.00 and up	1% of transaction value plus 20¢ per share

In addition, you may get slight discounts on orders involving more than $5,000:

Value of order	*Discount*
$5,000-$20,000	10%
$20,000-$40,000	20%

Above the level of $40,000, a special schedule exists, but you may be able to negotiate with your broker for an additional discount beyond the scheduled one. Of course, your broker will have to be careful not to be caught by one of the exchanges, or his livelihood may be in jeopardy.

That's right. The Canadian broker is not allowed to cut commission rates, because they are fixed by a cartel consisting of the various stock exchanges and the brokerage community.

Let's look at some numerical examples, to see how high commissions can be. Say you buy 25 shares at $10⅛ per share. Total cost of the shares is $253.125. The commission you pay is $6.31, or 2.5%. A similar commission of 2.5% would be due if you sold your shares for 15% more than you bought them. In other words, the commission would take out a full 33% of your profit *before* taxes.

Let us look at a "mixed order." Suppose you bought 500 shares, composed of 200 shares at $5 per share and 300 shares at $5¼ per share. Total cost of the shares: $2,575. The commission? $76.50, or 3% — even higher than before. Here, you may lose 6% in the buy/sell process, or 40% of that 15% return. Consider now a large transaction. Say you buy 5,000 shares at $10 per share. Total cost: $50,000. Your commission expense: $962.50, or about 2%. This is after taking advantage of the "volume discount"; even so, it is still a lot of money.

It is probably becoming clear just how high brockerage commissions in Canada are. In Germany or Switzerland, for example, they are about one-half or even one-third of the Canadian level. As for the U.S., its brokerage community used to have the same type of cartel that exists in Canada. However, a few years ago, the U.S. Congress decided to intervene in that last stronghold of price fixing and "open up" the field for competition. Brokers, of course, complained bitterly. Several of them even went out of business, and others merged with larger brokerage houses. But there arose a type of broker who provides the same type of service as the regular ones, but at *less than half* the price. These are "discount brokers."

Regular brokers claim, with some justification, that their high commissions are necessary to pay for "research"; that is, to retain a number of analysts who follow stocks and brief the brokers. Then, when you, the customer, ask for investment advice, the broker may advise you correctly. In other words, half your commission goes toward research, whether you use the research or not. Is it worth it? If you prefer to make up your own mind about your investments, you would probably agree to dispense with your broker's advice — if you could only cut his commission in half.

Well, you can do this, provided you buy the shares you want outside Canada. If the company, whose shares you want to buy, is traded on one of the U.S. exchanges — the NYSE, the American Exchange, the OTC (over the counter), or one of the regional exchanges — then any U.S. discount broker would love to have your business. Remember that many Canadian stocks are traded on these U.S. exchanges, as well as on the Canadian exchanges. A U.S. discount broker will provide all the services that you now receive from your regular broker, except investment advice. The discount broker will provide margin accounts; pay you interest on the cash in your account; and automatically assign dividends to your account. And, best of all, he will charge you less than half the rates you would have paid if you bought the same stock in Canada (although he may charge a minimum on very small orders). Of course, only the largest of Canadian companies trade on the U.S. exchanges, but the number is not insignificant.

So how do you open an account with a U.S. discount broker? Simple. Just call him or her and you will be quoted an account number. Once you send a cheque by mail and deposit some money in your account, you are in business. Remember, though, that the cheque should be in U.S. dollars. You can rest assured that your savings on commissions will easily pay for the long-distance calls you make when placing your buy/sell orders.

Let us now look, for comparison purposes, at some typical U.S. commission rates. Even the most expensive firms such as Merrill Lynch are cheaper on the average than Canadian firms. These rates, shown in the table below, are approximations only, since the rates change constantly with changing competitive forces. We have chosen some sample share purchases and calculated the commission for each one, in percentage points as well as in dollars. You can compare these with the Canadian rates quoted previously, and to the discount broker's rate quoted at the bottom of the table.

	300 shares @$16/share	500 shares @$18/share	1,000 shares @$14/share	5,000 shares @$17/share
Merrill Lynch:	$108.00 (2.3%)	$175.00 (1.9%)	$280.00 (2.0%)	$660.00 (0.8%)
Bache:	$110.35 (2.3%)	$181.75 (2.0%)	$288.00 (2.1%)	$666.00 (0.8%)
*Kingsley, Boye & Southwood:	$46.00 (1.0%)	$82.59 (0.9%)	$129.16 (0.9%)	$241.45 (0.3%)

*Discount Broker

Now, where do you find these discount brokers? Look through the pages of any U.S. financial publication, such as *Barron's, Forbes, The Wall Street Journal,* and so on. You will find more than you need. To make the task easier, here are the names of three brokers:

Kingsley, Boye & Southwood	Tel: (212) 480-1976
Icahn & Co.	Tel: (212) 483-0092
Muriel Siebert & Co.	Tel: (212) 248-0622

As a last comment, some of the brokers arrange for insurance on your account; that is, your investment may be protected against insolvency of the broker, in much the same way that U.S. bank depositors are protected by the Federal Deposit Insurance. Ask the broker about it, and he or she will be happy to tell you.

The Sexy Foreigners: buying shares abroad

In this section of the book on how to get a better-than-average return on investment, we've assumed that you will be putting your money into Canadian stocks. There is, however, no reason why you should restrict yourself to this relatively narrow range. Why not branch out and invest in stocks that are traded on a foreign exchange?

If you are like most people, your first reaction to this idea is probably to recoil at the prospect of dealing on a regular basis with a foreign broker who may be hundreds, or even thousands, of miles away from you. But your contact with him will be little different from your contact with a Canadian broker. You deposit funds into your account by sending a cheque in the mail, and you withdraw your profits (or dividends) by instructing your broker to send a cheque to you. Buy/sell orders are, of course, made over the phone.

Whether your broker is in, say, Toronto or New York, is immaterial. Your stock certificates are usually held by the broker for safekeeping anyway, and sending a cheque to New York (or receiving one) is the same as sending one to the downtown office of your Canadian broker. Also, if you can cut your commissions by more than half, which you can do, as we demonstrated in our last discussion, your savings will pay for your long-distance telephone calls.

You may, in fact, have been convinced by our discussion that it is possible to purchase many Canadian stocks on U.S. stock exchanges, and save a lot of money on commissions by using U.S. discount brokers. If so, then once you have taken a look at Canadian securities (both stocks and bonds) that are traded on the American stock exchanges, the next logical step is to look at American stocks and bonds that are traded there. The process is simple, and potentially profitable. And if you are prepared to consider investing in U.S. stocks and bonds, why not consider the European ones too?

You have no doubt wondered at times how to protect your Canadian dollars against inflation. One way is to "get into" a strong currency, such as the Swiss franc or the German mark. You could, for example, trade in foreign currency "futures" contracts. This is certainly one way to capitalize on currency changes, but it is extremely risky. Instead, you could consider investing in stocks and bonds that are denominated in foreign currencies. Purchasing a security denominated in a strong currency may give you dividends, which a straight purchase of foreign currency will not do. Also, it may provide you with capital appreciation through the performance of the company issuing the securities. And it may provide you with some gains on currency translation — if the dollar plunges against the currency of your choice. Naturally, these last two gains are not automatic: Appreciation of a stock's price is never guaranteed; nor is the exchange rate. But if you intended to buy, say, Swiss francs or German marks anyway, wouldn't it be a much better idea to buy Swiss franc- or German mark-denominated securities instead?

Now, how do you go about buying and selling European stocks and bonds? First of all, you should know that there are many hundreds of solid, publicly traded European companies whose securities you can invest in. Also, there are many reputable stock exchanges in Europe — London, Paris, Zürich, and Frankfurt being some of the best known ones. You should also know that not every European country lets you, a foreigner, buy and sell its securities freely. Yet there are still plenty of stocks and bonds you can buy.

There are even professional investment funds specializing in European securities ("Japan fund"— not a European fund, but still one based on foreign securities — has had a lot of success in recent years). Let us then look at six major European countries — France, Germany, Switzerland, the U.K., Italy and Sweden — and single out some points related to investments that you should be aware of.

France: Any foreigner may have a fully convertible account (*compte étranger*) with an authorized broker. You can buy and sell any French (or foreign) securities traded on the Paris "Bourse" at your leisure. You can buy any stock you want, that is, unless you attempt to take over a French company.

Germany: Since February 1, 1974, you have been able to buy any German security you desire, except money-market instruments (that is, treasury bills and similar federal interest-bearing, short-term notes), and German bearer bonds of less than four years' maturity. Bearer shares and bearer bonds do not require proof of identification upon redemption, and can therefore serve as a tax-evasion mechanism, which the Germans do not condone. You can buy any other type of German mark-denominated securities through any German bank, which can act as a broker. You will find their commission rates ridiculously low compared with Canadian rates.

Switzerland: Here you can buy only bearer shares, usually carrying inferior voting rights, or no voting rights at all. But since you are a foreigner, you are not allowed to influence the affairs of a public Swiss corporation anyway. At any rate, you probably only want to make a profit and do not much care about voting rights. And for purposes of dividends and capital appreciation, your bearer shares are as good as the "registered shares" held by Swiss nationals.

U.K.: Non-residents may freely purchase or sell all sterling-denominated securities. A small number of companies require all their shareholders to be British citizens, while a few others require a certain proportion of their shares to be held by British subjects. This latter rule is similar to the Canadian "constrained corporation" rule, and does not impede your investment unless you want to control the affairs of the company you have invested in.

Italy: Non-residents may buy and sell Italian securities freely, but the transaction must be made through an Italian bank. If you instruct any other broker to buy or sell an Italian security on an Italian stock exchange, this broker in turn would have to go through an Italian bank, thus doubling your commissions. Your securities may be kept with the Italian bank, or sent to you after being stamped *circolanto all'estero*.

Sweden: Aside from a law preventing foreigners from owning Swedish bank shares, there are few legal restrictions preventing you, as a foreigner, from buying Swedish securities. The few exceptions concern shares of some companies engaged in mining and real estate. Your Swedish broker could tell you about them in greater detail. There are also some rules preventing you from buying more than 20% of the voting rights or 40% of the total share capital of Swedish companies. This would not be relevant to you, we assume, unless you wanted to take over a Swedish company.

Some companies have separate "Class B" shares, usually with inferior voting rights. These trade at a discount to the "free" shares, but in some companies they are the only shares available to foreigners. Remittance of capital dividends and interest on your investments in "VPC" (stock market) shares are generally unlimited.

One immediate problem when trading abroad is, of course, the language and how to follow the market when all transactions take place in a foreign tongue. If you know one of the European languages, particularly German or French, it's easy: You can follow developments merely by reading the local financial press. But even if you are only conversant in English, there are still many avenues open to you for investing in Europe (or Japan, or Hong Kong, or Australia). For example, most large European brokers have liaisons with U.S. brokers. They supply both information and execution (transaction) services. So if you intend to invest in European stocks, you can contact one of the major brokers and be put in touch with a reputable broker in Europe.

A better approach is to open an account with one of the Swiss banks represented in Canada — we'll have more to say about them later. Your Swiss representative will be able to key you in to the investment department of his bank. And, as an added benefit, you will find that the commission rates of Swiss banks — and also of German banks — are pleasantly low: less than half the amount you would pay to a Canadian broker. Swiss and German banks are "total" banks, and can buy and sell stocks for you — something a Canadian bank cannot directly do. But you'll have to be careful: European banks will be happy to help you, and their commissions are low, but they will charge you for each and every service they perform for you. If you are investing large amounts of money, they may skip some of the charges or reduce them, but otherwise you should keep an eye on your costs.

Another way to obtain current information about European securities is to contact a leading broker who's located in the country in which you plan to invest. Say you intend to invest in British stocks and happen to be in London for a vacation, a business trip, or to visit your mother-in-law. Drop in on a broker; you'll find many of them clustered around the Stock Exchange. Open an account there. Have a chat with one of the customer-service people. Explain that you would like to invest in the market, and ask for some of their recommendations. Then ask to be put on their mailing list. Each and every brokerage house has some kind of communication going to its customers, with a summary of the market and events and select buy/sell recommendations. You could learn much merely by scanning this professional summary of the week (or the month) that was. Alternatively, you can always write from Canada and try to get on the mailing list without making a personal visit.

Now let us say a few words about currency effects. You have to remember that on top of the normal investment risk associated with buying stocks, you will run the risk of losing on the exchange rate when you want to sell your stock and realize any profit you have earned. But if the exchange rate moves in the right direction, you also stand to gain, and that's worth bearing in mind too.

For a start, it is a useful rule to remember that, in the long term, one currency depreciates against another at a rate equivalent to the difference in the rates of inflation in the two countries. For instance, if the U.S. rate of inflation is 13%, while Germany's is 4% and Switzerland's 2%, then the German mark will appreciate (long term) against the U.S. dollar at approximately 9% per year, while the Swiss franc will gain approximately 11% each year. This is a long-term trend, remember, after discounting normal fluctuations.

So, if you intend to invest in foreign stock markets, first study the inflationary trends of the countries you are interested in; next, arrange to obtain information about the country on a regular basis, and then form a contact with a good broker there — either directly, or through a Canadian broker or a representative of a European bank in Canada. Finally, be prepared to make sense out of European financial reports, which you'll need to study before you invest in European stocks. We've discussed annual reports already, so we won't repeat every word here. However, we will point out the main differences between Canadian annual reports and the annual reports in the six countries we mentioned. We'll start with the balance sheet items:

France: Fixed assets are carried on the books as in Canada and the U.S. — at cost, less depreciation. Inventories, however, are stated at the average cost, and not, as is the practice in North America, at the lower of cost or market (that is, an approximation of liquidation value). As for shares, you will find that French companies have only common shares. There are no preferred shares, although some securities are ingeniously structured to resemble them. Long-term liabilities also include special employee profit-sharing provisions, which in North America are usually relegated to the footnotes.

Germany: It's the same as in France, except that inventories are usually stated at the lower of cost or market. This is more conservative and therefore better. Also, preferred shares are available in German companies, and these are fully participatory in any liquidation proceedings — as are the common shares — but their voting rights are restricted. Long-term liabilities include provisions for pension liabilities. Again, this is better than in North America, where this often substantial item is banished to the footnotes.

Switzerland: Assets are sometimes carried on the books at the nominal value of one Swiss franc. This is done so that all the investment may be used in the first year as a tax-deductible expense. Assets therefore, appear slim, and reserves even slimmer. This picture, though, is highly misleading. Swiss companies, as a rule, are much better off than you may assume by glancing at their balance sheets. Shares include both voting and non-voting common stock. You, as a foreigner, would most often be restricted to the second type.

In general, it may be said that Swiss companies (and to a lesser degree, German ones) understate their true asset value. It is, therefore, possible to see Swiss and German companies trading on European stock markets at price/earnings multiples of more than double their Canadian and American counterparts.

U.K.: Among the European companies, U.K. ones are the most accurately reported. Some companies take the trouble to revalue *all* their assets at year-end. Others take into account the effects of inflation. This last practice — in the leading edge of accounting science — shows just how much of a company's earnings are real and how much are simply the result of inflation. Look up some U.K. companies' annual reports. Those using "inflation accounting" are highly instructive. Long-term liabilities also include reserves for "foreseeable" tax liabilities, which, in the U.K., is definitely prudent.

Italy: Companies generally report as in France and Germany, but the balance sheet of Italian firms also includes provisions for personnel termination indemnities. This, in labor-union Italy, is a must. There are also provisions for potential tax liabilities. All these provisions are desirable, since the book value of the company is, therefore, given net of all possible deductions. Of course, one must not overdo the reporting prudence game, as companies may seem to be worth much less than they really are — see **Switzerland**, above.

Sweden: Balance sheets are generally the same as in Germany and France, but inventories may be depreciated, thus creating another expense. This, in turn, reduces the income and therefore the tax bite. This, of course, is laudable, but causes an understatement of the true values of inventories and of the true level of income. If you know about the practice, though, you can allow for it. As we have mentioned before, shares come in two classes: A and B. A shares have voting rights, while B shares have only a fraction of the voting rights of the A shares. Long-term liabilities include tax-free reserves, and also pension liabilities. Both, in Sweden, are significant.

Let's now turn to the income statement items:

France: Sales and income figures are published, as in North America. Companies operating several businesses must provide a breakdown of sales by business areas. In Canada and the U.S., this is not always mandatory.

Germany: Sales and income figures are given as in North America.

Switzerland: In this haven of capitalism, many companies do not publish sales figures at all. Earnings, too, mostly understate the true profit picture. All investments, for instance, are written off (treated as expenses) in the year in which they are made. This turns them immediately into big tax deductions. The tax bite therefore is smaller, which contributes to the health of the company. But this practice understates the true income picture.

U.K.: Sales and income figures are as reported in the

U.S. and Canada, with a few minor variations. Inflation accounting, of course, makes a huge difference, just as it would in the case of North American companies.

Italy: Sales and income are published twice a year. Consolidated sales are given. These include sales of controlled subsidiaries, net of intercompany transactions.Income figures, however, are merely an indication of the level of profitability, since leeway in managing the reserves gives management an opportunity to smooth out earnings from one year to the next.

Sweden: Sales and income figures are given, but income includes part of the allocation to tax-free reserves. Thus, some of the reported income cannot be used to pay dividends without the company paying half of it to the tax collector.

In general, it may be said that among European companies with *similar financial appearance*, the Swiss companies are by far the best. We would not hesitate, though, to put German companies a close second.

Swiss Banks: how to do business with the gnomes

We mentioned in our last discussion that one of the best ways of investing in European stocks is through a Swiss bank. There are, however, a number of other reasons for opening an account with a Swiss bank — one of them being security. You'll sleep more peacefully at night.

Also, it makes sense to have some of your investments in a strong currency such as the Swiss franc, because of the economic truism we mentioned earlier: The long-term appreciation of one currency against another is roughly equivalent to the difference between the inflation rates generated by the governments issuing those currencies. In Switzerland, the rate of inflation is approximately 1½% per annum. In Canada, it is closer to 10% if you accept the government figures, or maybe 15% if you look at your grocery bills. The appreciation of the Swiss franc against the Canadian dollar would therefore be about 9%-14%, per annum. Of course, in the short term there would be fluctuations that might cause this rate to vary. But in the long run, this rate of appreciation would apply. Therefore, merely holding Swiss francs would give you adequate long-term protection against Canada's high inflation.

However, if you go and buy Swiss francs outright, you do not receive any interest on your money. But if you have a Swiss bank account, with your savings denominated in Swiss francs, then you will earn interest on your money. Fortunately, opening a Swiss bank account is easy; and it's cheap. There are no extra charges for an account with a Swiss bank. Swiss banks are like any other banks (except for some nice differences, which we shall discover in a moment). Also, it's not just South American politicians and Arab sheiks who have accounts there. Ordinary mortals have them too.

Let's look at some of the considerations for having a Swiss account. First of all, you may keep your Swiss account money in any currency, including, of course, Swiss francs. You have probably heard that the Swiss have tried to discourage foreigners from holding money in Swiss francs, and that there is a penalty of negative interest on Swiss franc-denominated accounts. This is not entirely true. You may hold up to the equivalent of S.Fr. 100,000 (about $70,000) in a non-interest-bearing chequing account in any Swiss bank, without penalty. You may also deposit up to the equivalent of S.Fr. 20,000 (about $14,000) in an interest-bearing savings account — denominated in Swiss francs if you wish — again without penalty.

It is the money of large corporations that the Swiss don't like. When large multinational companies shunt their money back and forth in order to make slim profits through currency speculation, the Swiss franc is damaged and the Swiss economy suffers. Individuals, though, are welcomed. You may open a chequing account with as little as S.Fr. 100, depending on the bank, and there would be no charge, other than normal banking charges, if you maintained a balance of at least S.Fr. 1,000. If you want to receive interest on your Swiss franc deposit, you may choose between short-term deposits, carrying about 1½% interest, or longer-term deposits, carrying up to 2½%. Here, there would be a small charge of approximately S.Fr. 12 per year (about $8). You may withdraw up to S.Fr. 5,000 per month from the 1½% interest-bearing account. And you would have to give a month's notice for withdrawals from the 2½% interest-bearing account. These interest rates are not impressive, but remember that you would also participate in the appreciation of the Swiss franc against the Canadian dollar. The interest you would receive on your Swiss franc deposits would be subject to a 35% Swiss withholding tax. But this tax would be partially recouped when you declared the interest income on your Canadian income tax form.

Now let's look at some of the other advantages of a Swiss account. First, in a country where the inflation rate is less than 2%, what would you say to a bond denominated in Swiss francs that pays a coupon of between 3% and 4%? Add that 4% to the appreciation of the currency, and you begin to realize the returns you can get on what is still a safe investment. Of course, not only can you hold Swiss francs in your account, but, as we indicated, you can also convert at your convenience to any other currency of your choice: Japanese yen, German marks, and so on.

Another advantage is the fact that a Swiss bank can act for you in many other matters. In Canada, a bank is allowed to serve you only in commercial matters; trust companies may provide you with estate and trust services and brokers act as your agents in transactions of securities. In Switzerland, banks can do all these things. For example, your Swiss bank may act on your behalf as a broker, if you want to buy Swiss franc-denominated securities. And after suffering high Canadian brokerage fees, you will find your Swiss bank fees ridiculously low.

Finally, there's the advantage of confidentiality. The Swiss constitution sees human liberty as being inextricably linked with human property and the freedom to possess it. The Swiss believe that your financial affairs are your own business — and nobody else's. In Canada, your friends may call the bank in which you deposit your money, and ask for a credit check. This is done routinely by credit agencies every day. The bank manager would divulge the approximate amount in your chequing account, the amount outstanding on your loan, and the promptness with which you are repaying it. The Swiss find this unthinkable. In Switzerland, a banker who divulges anything about your finances would spend a long period behind bars, which means that your Swiss bank account is a matter strictly between you and your banker. As for the "numbered," or so-called "anonymous," bank accounts, they are merely an internal administrative device intended to minimize the number of bank employees who know the identity of the depositor. Every Swiss bank account is covered by the Swiss banking secrecy laws.

As a result, Swiss bank accounts are open to abuse. Some of the potential abuses have included tax evasion (which is, of course, a criminal offence in Canada, though not in Switzerland), and the surreptitious acquisition of securities by corporate insiders. But as we all know, *every* tool may be used in a fashion for which it was not intended. The legitimate uses of an account with a Swiss bank are still numerous: the holding of foreign currency as a protection against inflation; participation in European stock markets with greater ease; and last but not least, the safety of your funds. It is claimed that even in a case of a third world war, Switzerland would remain intact. The reason? All world leaders have accounts there.

If you are more than routinely knowledgeable in business matters, you may try to deal with one of the smaller (the so-called "private") Swiss banks. However, if you are not as sophisticated as Swiss bankers are reputed to be, you would do better to stick with one of the "Big Three" banks. They all have offices in Toronto, and can be reached by calling the following numbers and asking for the representative: Union Bank of Switzerland (416) 863-6820; Swiss Bank Corporation (416) 865-0190; Credit Suisse (416) 364-5659.

Part 2
LEGAL
TAX AVOIDANCE

Cutting Your Taxes: how the pros do it

Although one of the key objectives of sound financial planning is to maximize your earnings, an equally important aim is to minimize your costs. And the biggest of these is taxes. In many cases, the best way to reduce your expenses is simply to lower your taxes as much as is legally possible — chances are, your tax bill is usually the largest bill you will face in any one year. Here, then, are some tax ideas that you can use to lighten your burden — ideas that the professionals use.

Income splitting. The first thing you should do is consider whether you may be able to save taxes by income splitting. Because tax rates increase with your income, it is obviously a good idea to transfer some of your earnings to family members who are in lower tax brackets, so that tax on the income will come off your high tax bill and be added to theirs. Here are some of the rules of the game.

If you wish to split income with your spouse, you can not simply *give* her or him income-earning investments or money to buy such investments. The Income Tax Act contains some special provisions, known as the "attribution rules," and income or capital gains from property transferred to your spouse will be attributed back to you and taxed in your hands. The attribution rules also apply to income from properties substituted for, or replacing property that has been transferred. A much better idea is to *lend* money to your spouse so that she may purchase investments. Your loan could be repayable on demand, or it could provide for reasonable repayment terms. If the loan is properly documented and is carried out *bona fide* — in a businesslike manner — you should be able to split your income. But you and your spouse must follow the written terms of the loan.

The tax saving can be significant. For example, a 56% taxpayer — someone in the second highest Ontario tax bracket — can typically save about $2,000 on a $6,000 interest-bearing investment by having it taxed in his wife's hands (assuming she has no other taxable income). It's also worth noting that the attribution rules do not apply to your spouse's *business income*. That is, you may give your spouse money to invest in her own business and rest assured that any income earned will be taxed in her hands, not yours. But make sure that the business venture is really a business and not merely a passive investment.

Although there used to be restrictions on splitting business income by employing your spouse or forming a partnership with him or her, individual partners or proprietors may now deduct salaries to a spouse, if paid after 1979. In addition, a husband and wife may split income by forming a partnership, effective for fiscal periods of the partnership ending after December 31, 1979. For example, if you are professional, you can now pay your spouse's salary for services performed for your practice. (A note of caution: Salaries paid to a spouse must be reasonable in relation to the services performed, which must be of a business nature such as bookkeeping or secretarial services — not minding the kids.) Similar rules apply to partnerships. For example, if the partnership has apparently been formed with income splitting in mind, the tax people can still reapportion partnership between the spouses to a reasonable amount.

The attribution rules are more lenient where children under 18 are involved. For example, if a child makes a capital gain (as opposed to earning income) from property you give him there will be no attribution; your child will pay tax on the capital gain at his or her marginal rates. Also, you may probably be able to split income if you employ your child or form a partnership with him, provided these arrangements are *bona fide* and reasonable. Better still, the attribution rules do not apply at all to children who are 18 years of age or over. However, if you give capital property to your children, either over or under 18, you are generally treated for tax purposes as if you had sold the property at its fair market value, with the result that any capital gains that have accrued up to that point will be taxed in your hands. Also, if you live in Quebec you should be aware of the possibility of provincial gift taxes being payable when property is given to someone other than your spouse. If you're unsure of what to do, remember that you can always *lend* your children money to make investments, with the same income-splitting results that apply to your spouse.

Canadian investment income deduction. Another thing you should do is make sure that your investments fully utilize the $1,000 Canadian investment income deduction. This deduction is based on the first $1,000 of qualifying Canadian investment income, net of related interest expenses. Qualifying investment income usually includes Canadian interest from non-related sources, taxable Canadian dividends, and taxable (one half of actual) capital gains from the sale of most Canadian securities. The tax people have given you the opportunity to make up to $1,000 of investment income tax-free. So you should take advantage of it. Obviously, the sooner you put your money to work in a given year, the better chance you have to fully utilize the deduction. At an 11% return, for example, an investment of $9,091 made on January 1 will fully utilize your deduction. If you wait until July 1, you will need $18,182 of capital to do the trick.

Many people often forget that their spouse is also eligible for his or her own Canadian investment-income deduction. In most cases, it is a good idea to make sure that your spouse has some qualifying income, as a result of income splitting or otherwise. Remember, too, that if your spouse can reduce the taxable income to zero by claiming the basic personal exemption (and/or other deductions that precede it on the T2 income tax return), without having to claim the full investment-income deduction, then you may usually claim the unused portion.

Timing your interest expenses. Minimizing your taxable income is often only half the battle. What about your deductions? Every year, Canadian investors throw out millions of dollars in taxes because they incur non-deductible interest expenses. This arises from financing personal property purchases while having unleveraged income-earning investments. Whenever you have a personal debt at the same time as income-producing property that is fully paid for, you can save taxes. The key is to arrange the timing of your financial affairs so that your borrowings are against income-producing assets, not personal-use property. This is because interest expense is only deductible if the purpose of the loan is to make income.

Suppose, for example, that you purchased $2,500 worth of shares, and, at about the same time, bought a $1,000 color TV, borrowing $900 to do so. The interest on your loan would not be deductible. If, instead, you had borrowed the $900 to buy shares and had paid for the color TV in cash, then the interest on the loan would be deductible, and you would have obtained a valuable tax saving. The biggest waste of tax deductions in this area occurs when interest is being paid on a mortgage, while a taxpayer holds investments that have been fully paid for.

We'll have more to say about this in our next chapter. For now, let's just say that the smart, tax-planning point is that it's better not to get into this situation in the first place: If you anticipate having large personal expenditures requiring financing, such as buying a house or a car, it is better to borrow money to purchase your investments and pay the personal expenses in cash. This is a rule that you should always try to follow.

Tax shelters. Tax shelters such as Registered Retirement Savings Plans are available from numerous financial institutions, including banks, trust and insurance companies. Provided that your contributions do not exceed the allowable yearly limits, you will obtain immediate tax deductions for contributions made to an RRSP; in other words, you will pay no tax in the year on money that you contribute to the plan. Also, while your investment earns income inside the RRSP, there will be no immediate tax. Although amounts you take out of the plan will generally be taxable, the fact that you've had untaxed income working for you should leave you ahead of the game in the long run. This is the basic principle behind most tax shelters. And since those shelters should play such a key role in your investment program we have devoted separate discussions to the ones that are most important.

Not All Income is Equal: how the taxman plays favorites

Up to now we've made an unspoken assumption that all your investment income will be taxed in the same way. But as we have pointed out elsewhere, this is not always the case. Some income types are taxed much more favorably than others. Clearly it pays to maximize those income types and minimize the others. None of this negates our earlier discussion. It just adds another dimension. It will, for example, help you to decide which type of investment you should be making in the first place, since the different alternatives can have vastly different after-tax results. So let's have a look at some of the ground rules of the way different types of investment income are taxed, because a basic understanding of these rules will invariably mean more money in your pocket.

General rule. The general rule that applies to all investment income is that on every additional dollar you earn, you will be taxed at your marginal tax rate. Because tax rates increase with your taxable income, simply taking an average, dividing your tax by your taxable income, would underestimate the tax you would pay on those extra dollars of income. If you're in a 40% tax bracket, you will, in most cases, receive 60 cents on your investment dollar after tax. In other words, if you have a 10% investment, 4% will be taxed away, leaving you with a return of 6%. This basic rule applies to investments that yield interest, as well as to business and employment income. But like most other things, it's the exceptions to the rule that make life interesting. So let's look at these.

Capital gains. Instead of an investment that generates interest, you may wish to buy one that generates a capital gain. A dollar of capital appreciation is worth more after tax than a dollar of interest income. This is because only half your capital gains are taxable. So if your investment were to appreciate by 10%, only one-half — or 5% — would have to be included in your taxable income. Thus, our 40% bracket taxpayer would pay only 2% tax (40% of 5%) on the appreciation, and he would end up with an 8% after-tax return instead of the 6% we saw before.

Of course, many investments are taxed in more than one way. For example, bonds yield interest that is taxed in the "normal" manner, but a capital gain or loss may be in store if you sell the bond for a price other than the one you paid. The same applies to gains on stocks; however, as we will see shortly, different rules exist for dividends received from taxable Canadian corporations.

Since half of your capital gains are taxable, you would think that half of your capital losses (referred to as allowable capital losses) would be deductible. Instead, allowable capital losses are *fully* deductible — but only against taxable capital gains. In addition, however, up to $2,000 per year in excess allowable capital losses may be deducted against your other sources of income. Any remainder can then be applied to your previous year's income in a similar way. And if you still have capital losses left over, you may then apply them to the future year's income. One thing you should note is that buying an investment which may appreciate does not necessarily result in capital gain (or loss) treatment. If you have a gain or loss from the sale of non-capital property, the tax consequences will be calculated in the "normal" manner. Sometimes, the distinction between non-capital and capital property is not that simple. Partly it depends on the type of investment — for example, stocks are more likely to be classed as capital property than is vacant land that is held for speculative purposes.

But the tax people may also consider other factors, such as whether your investments are of the income-earning type (e.g. a bond is more likely to be a capital asset than a commodity); whether your buying and selling has the hallmarks of a business operation; and whether it is apparent that you intend to hold the property as an investment, rather than make a quick profit from its resale. If this sounds confusing, that's because it *is* confusing. But millions of tax dollars have been saved by people who challenged the tax department's opinions in court, and won. As a result, we'll have a lot more to say about this in our next discussion.

Two other things to note. A capital gain is usually determined by taking the difference between your proceeds of disposition and the total of your cost and selling expenses. But if you acquired capital property before 1972, special rates will apply. The second thing is that foreign property is eligible for capital gains treatment.

Dividends. Dividends (whether from common, preferred, or other types of shares) from taxable Canadian corporations are taxed in a rather special way, known as the "gross-up and credit system." This system has some important features. For every dollar of dividends you receive from a taxable Canadian corporation, you must add 50 cents to your taxable income (the gross-up). But in return for this inconvenience, you get to take a little over 50 cents (this varies from province to province) off your tax bill. This is the dividend tax credit. When you sort it all out, you will see that it's a good deal. That's because no matter what tax bracket you are in, you will pay less tax on the 50 cents you have to add on, than you get back from the dividend tax credit. Not only that, but the lower the tax bracket you're in, the less tax you will have to pay on the 50 cents gross-up — but you will still get the same tax credit. So, the lower your taxable income, the more you should favor dividends as opposed to other types of investment income.

Let's return to our example of the 40% bracket taxpayer. If he received a $100 dividend, his tax calculation would be as follows:

Dividend:	$100
Gross-up (50% of $100):	50
Taxable dividend:	$150
Tax (40% of $150):	$60
Less dividend tax credit (approx.):	50
Net tax:	$10
After-tax return ($100 - $10):	$90

This compares with an after-tax return of $60 from $100 of interest income, and $80 from an investment that yields $100 of capital-gains income. So you can see that it usually pays to earn dividend income first, then capital gains and then interest income. There is, however, one exeption to this. Dividends paid in stock by Canadian public companies, foreign source dividends and dividends from tax-deferred shares are not subject to these rules.

Now that we've dealt with the ground rules, take a look at the table below. It provides some key figures that you may use to determine your after-tax return per dollar of investment income. The table shows taxes on ordinary income (for example, interest), dividends from taxable Canadian companies, and capital gains. It also shows the amount of ordinary income required to match one dollar of dividends on an after-tax basis. When examining the table, note the following:

* Capital gains and dividends will always yield better tax results than interest or other income taxed in the "normal" manner.
* Except for the top two tax brackets (top three in Quebec), dividends are taxed more favorably than capital gains.

* Taxpayers with taxable income less than $19,866 receive dividends tax-free (except in Quebec). Persons making less than $16,254 will actually get a tax refund if they receive Canadian source taxable dividends.

Comparative tax rates for dividends, capital gains and ordinary income
(brackets denote tax saving)

1980 Taxable Income:	$12,642 -16,254	$16,254 -19,866	$19,866 -25,284	$25,284 -43,344	$43,344 -70,434	$70,434 -108,360	$108,360 +
British Columbia and Ontario							
Dividends	(4.05)%	nil %	6.08%	15.12%	23.76%	30.24%	38.88%
Ordinary income	31.05	33.75	37.80	46.08	51.84	56.16	61.92
Capital gains	15.53	16.88	18.90	23.04	25.92	28.08	30.96
After tax return dividends/ordinary income	1.51	1.51	1.51	1.57	1.58	1.59	1.61
Alberta							
Dividends	(3.89)	nil	5.83	14.54	22.85	29.09	37.4
Ordinary income	29.78	32.37	36.26	44.32	49.86	54.02	59.55
Capital gains	14.89	16.19	18.13	22.16	24.93	27.01	29.78
After tax return dividends/ordinary income	1.48	1.48	1.48	1.54	1.54	1.54	1.55
Saskatchewan							
Dividends	(4.32)	nil	6.48	16.06-16.62	26.12	33.24	42.74
Ordinary income	33.12	36.0	40.32	48.96-50.66	56.99	61.74	68.07
Capital gains	16.56	18.0	20.16	24.48-25.33	28.50	30.87	34.04
After tax return dividends/ordinary income	1.56	1.56	1.57	1.651.69	1.72	1.75	1.79
Manitoba							
Dividends	(4.35)	nil	6.53	16.17	25.41	32.34	41.58
Ordinary income	33.35	36.25	40.60	49.28	55.44	60.06	66.22
Capital gains	16.68	18.13	20.3	24.64	27.72	30.03	33.11
After tax return dividends/ordinary income	1.57	1.57	1.57	1.65	1.67	1.69	1.73
Quebec (see note 2)							
Dividends	5.27	10.46	15.29	22.18	33.10	41.29	46.30
Ordinary income	38.81	42.26	45.49	52.33	59.61	65.08	68.41
Capital gains	19.41	21.13	22.74	26.17	29.81	32.54	34.2
After tax return dividends/ordinary income	1.55	1.55	1.55	1.63	1.66	1.68	1.7
Nova Scotia and Prince Edward Island							
Dividends	(4.31)	nil	6.46	16.01	25.16	32.03	41.18
Ordinary income	33.0	35.87	40.18	48.80	54.90	59.48	65.57
Capital gains	16.5	17.94	20.09	24.4	27.45	29.74	32.79
After tax return dividends/ordinary income	1.56	1.56	1.56	1.64	1.66	1.68	1.71

New Brunswick							
Dividends	(4.30)	nil	6.45	16.01	25.15	32.02	41.16
Ordinary income	32.99	35.86	40.17	48.78	54.88	59.46	65.55
Capital gains	16.5	17.93	20.09	24.39	27.44	29.73	32.78
After tax return dividends/ordinary income	1.56	1.56	1.56	1.64	1.66	1.68	1.71
Newfoundland							
Dividends	(4.47)	nil	6.71	16.59	26.07	33.18	42.66
Ordinary income	34.27	37.25	41.72	50.56	56.88	61.62	67.94
Capital gains	17.14	18.63	20.86	25.28	28.44	30.81	33.97
After tax return dividends/ordinary income	1.59	1.59	1.60	1.69	1.72	1.74	1.79

Notes:

1. Nine percent federal tax reduction included in first three columns.
2. Quebec rates at lower end of tax bracket used with an additional $1,670 subtracted from taxable income to give effect to higher personal exemptions applicable to a married person with no children.
3. For Saskatchewan, second figure in third column is applicable if taxable income exceeds $31,600.
4. Tax rates on dividends apply to taxable dividends from companies.
5. P.E.I. figures assume 52.5% rate applicable to entire year.

Canadian investment income. One qualification to the above rules that you might find important is the Canadian investment income deduction that we mentioned in our last discussion. If you earn types of income that are eligible for this deduction, you may be entitled to an offsetting deduction of up to $1,000. In other words, to the extent that the income qualifies for this deduction, it will be received tax-free. In most cases, you calculate your deduction by first taking the total of:

* eligible interest income, generally from a Canadian source;
* taxable amounts of dividends from Canadian corporations (this is 1½ times the actual cash dividend you receive);
* taxable (half of actual) capital gains from most Canadian securities.

Then you subtract:

* deductible interest expenses that you incurred to earn the first two types of income mentioned above.

However, remember that the maximum deduction you are entitled to take is $1,000. This deduction can be very important when calculating your after-tax return. You will find that in many cases it will make a qualifying investment more attractive than an investment that is not eligible for the Canadian investment income deduction. For example, Canadian dividends eligible for this deduction nevertheless qualify for the dividend tax credit. In this case a dollar of dividends will generate a tax reduction of slightly more than 50 cents.

Although the rules discussed above are simple enough, bear in mind that many sophisticated investments are merely variations on these themes. If you understand the basics, you will be well on your way to being able to cope with more complicated tax planning ideas.

A Capital Idea: making sure your gains qualify

Almost every investor knows that it's a good idea to have capital-gains treatment on the sale of any investment, because then only half of the profit will be taxable. But equally important is to determine when you qualify for a capital gain. There are two reasons for saying this. First, a firm idea about your potential tax liability will help you determine the investments that are right for you. For example, if you're in a 50% tax bracket, a 12% fully taxable investment will yield only 6% after tax, while an investment yielding just 9% in capital gain will net you 6¾% after tax (since the tax will be 50% of one-half of 9%). Second, you will be able to deal with your investments so that you will meet as many of the criteria for capital gains as possible. That means, for example, that your correspondence and other documentation can be worded to emphasize factors that will help your case, and de-emphasize factors that won't.

Unfortunately, though, the distinction between a capital and a non-capital property is not all that simple. The same type of asset may be capital to one person, but non-capital to another. And sometimes it is possible for the same asset to be capital and then non-capital to the same person at different times. The criteria for determining whether the sale of your investment will qualify for capital gains treatment have been established by a large number of court cases over the years. And the crucial question these cases have considered is this: Is the sale itself part of your overall profit-making scheme (in which case the gain will be fully taxable); or are you merely realizing on your capital, which itself is used to generate income (in which case capital-gains treatment will apply)? Although this sounds simple enough, it's not that black and white when a particular sale is analyzed. The tax people will look for certain factors that can make or break your case for capital treatment.

Before we discuss them in detail, bear in mind that these factors should be considered as a whole. In most cases, some will work in your favor and some won't. But since it's the total picture that matters here, don't be put off by those that work against you.

Factor 1: Did you earn income from the investment? Some types of assets, such as commercial real estate, stocks, bonds, and the like, produce investment income in the form of rents, dividends, interest and so on. Others, such as commodities, currency, and vacant land, by their very nature may produce no income at all. Generally, the likelihood of successfully claiming capital-gains treatment when you sell is greater with investments that can produce income (although this may depend upon the type of income involved). For example, unless you are very active in the market you should not have too much trouble with securities such as stocks and bonds, even if dividends are few and far between. However, certain types of real estate investments will be trickier. Parking-lot operations have been subject to close scrutiny, and so, too, have apartments. Frequent dealings in discounted mortgages have also been suspect.

Contrary to popular belief, however, the fact that an investment does not generate income does not necessarily mean that you won't be able to claim capital-gains treatment. Commodities are a good example. Revenue Canada generally gives you the option of claiming capital or income treatment for commodity transactions, as long as you are consistent. You might ask: Why claim income treatment if the advantages of capital treatment are so great? The answer is that, with income treatment, your losses are fully deductible from income. In contrast, only one-half of your capital losses — referred to as allowable capital losses — are deductible. And even then, there are restrictions on the losses you can claim. Allowable capital losses are fully deductible against taxable capital gains (that is, half of actual capital gains), but deductions of any excess allowable capital losses are hard to come by. In any year, you may deduct only up to $2,000 of excess allowable capital losses (half of actual capital losses) against other sources of income.

In addition, other non-income-producing investments may frequently qualify for capital-gains treatment, if the factors discussed below are strongly in your favor. This is especially true for objects that can be used for personal purposes, such as art, rare coins or land that is held for recreation or retirement.

Factor 2: Is it apparent that your main intention was to make a quick profit? The fact that you actually make money from your investment does not necessarily get you out of the woods. If the evidence indicates that you always intended to make a profit on its resale, you will be in trouble, regardless of what you do with the property in the meantime. The problem is that, as a prudent investor, you will almost always have had the possibility of a profitable resale in the back of your mind. But like everything else, it's a question of degree. You must try to show the tax people that turning the asset around for a profit was not a major motive in your investment decision. How do you do this? Evidence of refusal to sell in the face of offers helps. With real estate investments, for example, your case will be helped by architect's drawings, negotiations with potential tenants, suitable zoning bylaws and other evidence of attempts to develop your property into a long-term investment. But one of the most effective ways is simply to hold onto your investments.

Factor 3: How long have you owned the investment? Generally speaking, the longer you hold an investment, the better your case will be. However, no matter how long you have owned it, the tax people may argue that, even though you originally made the purchase for investment or personal reasons, your motives have since changed. This often happens when an investor attempts to subdivide land prior to sale. The tax people say they will go easy on subdivisions, when either farmland or inherited land is involved, but even here you're treading on thin ice, especially if other indications of speculative activities are there.

However, the fact that an investment was once held for speculative purposes does not taint it forever — if, for example, it is inherited by a person who intends to hold it as an investment. But this can work in reverse, especially when an inherited investment, which was formerly held for investment purposes. is sold off quickly after it is received.

Factor 4: Have you bought and sold other investments of the same type? Of course, even taxpayers with the best of intentions are often in jeopardy if they have bought and sold the same type of investment a number of times. But even if you're in this situation, all is not lost. You may be able to show that the circumstances of a particular sale were somehow different from the others — for example, if the sale occurred a long time before or after other sales.

Conversely, even if your sale is an isolated transaction, this does not necessarily mean you're off the hook. In many instances, when it is apparent that you intended to earn a profit on your one and only sale, or were engaged in what amounts to a business venture, the gain will be taxable, especially if a quick turnover is involved. The way to stay out of this trap is to avoid, in every way possible, giving the impression that you're using the same methods to make money on the resale as a sophisticated speculator would.

Factor 5: Do the circumstances of the sale indicate you are in the business of buying and selling? This brings us to another important factor — the circumstances of your sale. You should try to show that you were not actively trying to sell your investment in a sophisticated manner by large-scale advertising, or by attempts to put it into a more marketable condition just prior to sale. The magic phrase that keeps cropping up in successful tax cases is "unsolicited offer," especially for real-estate sales. Another successful strategy is to demonstrate that there was a change in conditions, which frustrated your original intention to develop or to hold your investment. Some factor that may result in "frustrated intentions" are unforeseen costs or expenses; events that are not compatible with your intended use; a falling-out with your partners or co-venturers; ill health; inadequate return on your investment.

Factor 6: Is the transaction closely related to your regular business? Another key is the relationship of your investment activities to your regular occupation. For example, lawyers may find themselves in trouble over mortgage sales, and stockbrokers may be in trouble with the purchase and sale of securities. However, these taxpayers have sometimes been able to show that such properties were purchased for investment or personal, rather than business-related, purposes.

Because of the problems in distinguishing between capital and non-capital investments, the tax people allow you to make a lifetime election to treat dispositions from most Canadian securities as capital gains or losses — provided you are not a trader or dealer in securities. Canadian securities (other than those acquired in a non-arm's-length transaction) on which this election can be made are:

* Shares of Canadian resident corporations.
* Bonds, debentures, mortgages or other similar obligations issued by a person resident in Canada.

However, there are a few exceptions, notably:

* Shares of a non-public company, the value of which is primarily attributable to real estate.
* Certain shares of resource companies, which allow the shareholder to write off the company's exploration and development expenses.
* Debt obligations of a non-public corporation, which is not at arm's length with the taxpayer at any time prior to the disposition.

But before you lock yourself in forever, remember the restrictions on capital losses discussed above. Should your investment program falter, you may wish to argue that your losses are fully deductible. However, if you have made an election for capital treatment you won't be able to do this.

But even if you don't want to lock yourself in, there

are still some opportunities for using the election. It may be possible, for example, to have securities purchased by a corporation or a family member so that they can make a lifetime election. Although there are some general anti-tax-avoidance rules aimed at this sort of manoeuvre, your tax adviser may feel it's worth a shot, especially if a lot of money is involved.

When Companies Eat Themselves: how to join the free lunch

Every year, a number of public Canadian companies buy back their own shares — usually because they decide to go private, they are taken over, or they merge. Whenever this happens, there is a good opportunity for you to make some major tax savings — if you buy into the company before the company buys back its shares. Fortunately, it is quite easy to do this, since decisions by companies to buy back their shares are usually taken with plenty of advance notice. Your broker will be able to keep you up-to-date on such developments. And we strongly recommend that you ask him to do so — that is, ask him to tell you when a buy-back opportunity is about to arise. You will find that the tax savings involved are so great that many investors are willing to pay a premium for the buy-back shares. This is particularly true for investors in low tax brackets, since the lower your bracket, the greater your saving.

This is how it all works. If a Canadian company acquires its own shares for a price that exceeds the original issue price, then certain tax rules treat part of the buy-back price as an "artificial" dividend — in this case called a "deemed dividend" — and create an offsetting capital loss. To be precise, the difference between the acquisition price and the paid-up capital per share is a deemed dividend. The capital loss is the difference between the cost of the shares for tax purposes and the paid-up capital. But that's just for accountants to worrry about. The reason this is so lucrative is that, for lower bracket shareholders, the capital losses are worth more in terms of tax savings than the tax that must be paid on the dividends. One of the main reasons for this is that the dividend tax credit is available to offset the tax you must pay on the dividends.

To calculate how much you personally can benefit from these buy-back shares, you have to calculate the tax effects of the dividend and the capital loss. Because these depend on the tax bracket you're in, we can't generalize. However, we have prepared the table shown below, which shows the taxes on dividends and capital gains (or losses) for different tax brackets in all ten provinces. You can use this table to calculate your tax saving.

Comparative percentage tax rates for dividends and capital gains
(brackets denote tax saving)

1980 Taxable income:	$12,642 -16,254	$16,254 -19,866	$19,866 -25,284	$25,284 -43,344	$43,344 -70,434	$70,434 -108,360	$108,360 plus
British Columbia	%	%	%	%	%	%	%
- Dividend	(4.05)	nil	6.08	15.12	23.76	30.24	38.88
- Capital gains	15.53	16.88	18.90	23.04	25.92	28.08	30.96
Alberta							
- Dividend	(3.89)	nil	5.83	14.54	22.85	29.09	37.40
- Capital gains	14.89	16.19	18.13	22.16	24.93	27.01	29.78
Saskatchewan							
- Dividend	(4.32)	nil	6.48	16.06-16.62	26.12	33.24	42.74
- Capital gains	16.56	18.00	20.16	24.48-25.33	28.50	30.87	34.04
Manitoba							
- Dividend	(4.35)	nil	6.53	16.17	25.41	32.34	41.58
- Capital gains	16.68	18.13	20.30	24.64	27.72	30.03	33.11
Ontario	See British Columbia. The same figures apply.						

Quebec (see note 3)							
- Dividend	5.27	10.46	15.29	22.18	33.10	41.29	46.30
- Capital gains	19.41	21.13	22.74	26.17	29.81	32.54	34.20
Nova Scotia and Price Edward Island							
- Dividend	(4.31)	nil	6.46	16.01	25.16	32.03	41.18
- Capital gains	16.50	17.94	20.09	24.40	27.45	29.74	32.79
New Brunswick							
- Dividend	(4.30)	nil	6.45	16.01	25.15	32.02	41.16
- Capital gains	16.50	17.93	20.09	24.39	27.44	29.73	32.78
Newfoundland							
- Dividend	(4.47)	nil	6.71	16.59	26.07	33.18	42.66
- Capital gains	17.14	18.63	20.86	25.28	28.44	30.81	33.97

Notes:

1. 9% federal tax reduction included in first three columns.
2. For low tax brackets, the tax savings from buy-back shares will differ slightly from result calculated in tables.
3. Quebec rates at lower end of tax bracket used, with an additional $1,670 subtracted from taxable income, to give effect to higher personal exemptions applicable to a married person with no children.
4. If you wish to determine the tax rate applicable to ordinary income (such as interest) multiply the capital gains rates by two.

Here's how to do it:

1. Ask your broker for the amount of the deemed dividend per share. (This will vary, depending on the shares.) Then look at the table and from the first row for your province, calculate the tax you must pay on the dividend. Note that for low tax brackets you may actually get a tax saving, because of the dividend tax credit.
2. Subtract the deemed dividend from the buy-back price. Then subtract this result from the price you pay for the share — including brokerage fees. (Alternatively, you can subtract the paid-up capital of the buy-back share from the price you pay.) This will give you your capital loss per share. Then use the table again, and from the second row for your province, calculate the tax savings resulting from the capital loss.
3. Add the results of the first two steps to give you your total tax saving per share.

4. If you have to pay a premium over the buy-back price, subtract the premium from the tax savings.
5. Multiply your net savings per share by the number of shares that will be bought back by the company. This will give you your total savings.

All of this is fairly complicated, so let's look at an example — the recent buy-back that occurred for the shares of Skyline Hotels Ltd. In this particular case, Skyline was to acquire its shares at $5.50 each and the demand dividend was $5.49 per share. Let's assume you are a B.C. resident with a taxable income of $21,000. Here's how you would calculate your saving if you had bought 500 Skyline shares at, say, $5.75 — at a premium.

* Using the table, and the 6.08% rate applicable in this example to dividends, you can see that the amount of tax you would have to pay per share on the deemed dividend would be 6.08% fo $5.49, or 33 cents per share.
* The difference between the buy-back price and the deemed dividend is one cent. Subtracting this from the $5.75 price per share gives you a capital loss per share of $5.74. The tax benefit in this particular situation is $18.9% of $5.74, or $1.08 per share.
* Thus the total tax saving per share would be $1.08 minus 33 cents, or 75 cents per share.
* Subtracting the 25 cents premium per share from your tax savings gives you a net return of 50 cents per share.
* Multiplying this by your 500 share purchase gives you an overall after-tax return of $250 on your investment of $2,875.

This is an excellent return, considering that you would get your money back from the company shortly after the buy-back.

There are a few other things to note about purchasing buy-back shares. As we said, the lower your tax bracket, the bigger your tax savings will be. Conversely, the higher your bracket, the lower your savings. And, as you can imagine, there comes a time when there are no savings at all. If you look at the table, you will see that in the top two brackets (three in Quebec), the tax rate on the dividend exceeds the taxes saved on the capital loss. This means that if you are in these tax brackets, it's a mistake to purchase buy-back shares.

In many cases, too, not all of your shares will be bought back. And sometimes the exact percentage that will be bought back will not be known until the deal has gone through. In these cases you must calculate the tax effects of the buy-back using only the estimated number of shares that will be purchased by the company. The remainder of the shares will have to be sold on the open market, *without* the tax breaks we've described. Because of this, it may be a good idea to look only for deals that involve a 100% buy-back.

Also, if you're considering a large purchase of buy-back shares, bear in mind that there is a restriction on the amount of capital losses (resulting from the buy-back or otherwise) that can be claimed in any one year. Although capital losses are fully deductible against capital gains, a maximum of $4,000 of capital losses can be claimed against other sources of income in any one year (in Quebec, the limit is $2,000). If your capital losses exceed this year's allowable deductions, any remainder can be applied against taxable capital gains in your previous year's return — first, against net capital gains, and then a further $4,000 ($2,000 in Quebec) against other sources of income, less any allowable capital losses deducted in the previous year. (To do this, obtain Form T1A from your District Taxation Office.) If allowable capital losses are still left over after the one year carry-back, you can apply them to future tax returns, in the same amounts. In this case, you will have to wait to receive the tax benefits from your capital losses.

But you will have to pay tax on the deemed dividend in the year of the buy-back.

You can create any size capital loss you wish, simply by dividing the desired capital loss by the capital loss per share. The quotient will be the number of shares you need to purchase. One thing that is not well known is that Revenue Canada may be able to nullify part or all of the tax benefits from the transaction (particularly the capital losses), especially if you buy in just before the company acquires its own shares. Although there has been no indication that it is inclined to do so, you should keep this possibility in mind, especially if a large purchase is planned.

RRSPs: your spouse may be worth more than you think

Financial security on your retirement, as indeed at any other time, means having enough income to maintain the standard of living to which you have become accustomed. Since income can only come from two sources — employment, or from accumulated assets — and since, when you retire, you have no employment income, your financial security then depends only on your assets. That's why it is so important to accumulate assets during your working years — and the more you can accumulate the better.

If you are like most Canadians you probably acquire the bulk of your assets using after-tax dollars — that is, the income you earn from your employment on which you have already been taxed. If you could accumulate assets with money that would normally go to the government in taxes, then obviously you would be much further ahead. This is the basis of the appeal of tax shelters in general, and of the most popular shelter of all — the Registered Retirement Savings Plan, or RRSP. The table below shows just how much difference investing pre-tax dollars can make to someone who is 35 years old and planning to retire at age 65. With an RRSP, you will end up $65,965 ahead of the person without an RRSP. We assume here that in both cases — for the investor with an RRSP and for the investor without — the amount of money saved each year is the same, and so, too, is the rate of return (a modest 8%).

Comparison of RRSP and non-RRSP returns on the same investment

	Non-RRSP	**RRSP**
Age:	35	35
Tax bracket:	40%	40%
Pre-tax amount available each year:	$1,000	$1,000
Tax paid on above:	400	NIL
Net amount available for investment:	600	1,000
Rate of return on investment:	8%	8%
Balance after 1st year:	648	1,080
Pre-tax amount available over 30-year period:	30,000	30,000
Net amount invested:	18,000	30,000
Tax paid during 30-year period:	8,775*	NIL
Net return on investment:	38,380	92,345
Value of retirement fund (principal & interest):	$56,380	122,345

* Assume 40% tax payable on all "interest" in excess of $1,000 in any year.

You may have heard people say RRSPs are not for everyone. This may be true in some cases, but if you are a taxpayer in Canada and saving any money at all, you owe it to yourself at least to examine them. Your failure to do so may cost you thousands of dollars in lost tax savings, even in the short term.

Contribution limits. First of all, how much can you pay into an RRSP? Basically your contribution limit depends on the size of your earned income, which you can calculate as follows:

Add your income from these sources — salary or wages; professional income (net); private pension income; Canada Pension Plan; and Old Age Security. Then subtract from this total the sum of your employment expense deduction (that is, 3% of your salary or wages, up to a maximum of $500); your unemployment insurance premiums and benefits; and your union and/or professional dues. This will give you your total earned income for RRSP purposes. To determine your contribution limit based on this total, you must then decide which of the following two groups of taxpayers you fall into: If you are an employee and a member of a pension plan, then your contribution limit is 20% of your earned income to a maximum of $3,500, *minus* your personal contribution (if any) to your pension plan. If you are an employee with no pension plan, or if you are self-employed, then your contribution limit is 20% of your earned income to a maximum of $5,500.

Pension income and other "rollovers." Although we said you can include any pension income in your earned income when calculating your contribution limit, there is an alternative course open to you, as follows: All or part of your private pension can be rolled over, or transferred directly into your RRSP (regardless of your contribution limit). This rollover can also be made with all or part of your Canada Pension and Old Age

Security. If you have taken early retirement (and are not yet 71 years old) and have then started a second career or another job, you may find it worthwhile to roll over your pension — particularly if the income now coming into your home exceeds your immediate needs. A retiring allowance, in whole or in part, can also be rolled over tax-free into your RRSP.

Rollovers do not affect the contribution limits outlined above. However, if you roll over any pension income you must not include the rolled-over funds in your earned income calculation. Incidentally, the first $1,000 of private-pension income is tax-free and should be taken into income each year. You can then roll over the balance. For example, if your private pension income is $9,000, it is a good idea to keep $1,000 tax-free and roll over the remaining $8,000.

Spousal RRSPs. Before you decide to make an RRSP contribution for yourself, you should first consider whether it is worth making one for your spouse. Under some circumstances this can be worthwhile. You are allowed to use all or part of your allowable contribution for your spouse instead of for yourself (apart from pension income and other rollovers), but for tax purposes you can still deduct the contribution from your own earned income. Funds can then accumulate in your spouse's name, even though she or he may have little or no income. The great advantage of a spousal RRSP is that when the plan matures (when your spouse is between the ages of 60 and 71), then the income will be taxed in your spouse's hands and not in yours, even though you made the contribution. Thus, if in retirement your spouse has less other income than you, you will be transferring the maturity income to the spouse in the lower tax bracket.

This income splitting can save you a significant amount of tax. But the saving doesn't end there. As we said above, the first $1,000 of private-pension income is tax free. This exemption also applies to maturity income from an RRSP (but only when your spouse reaches age 65). So if you have a private pension, and your spouse has an RRSP, then you both might qualify for a $1,000 exemption. This exemption, by the way, is in addition to the standard $1,000 Canadian interest income exemption.

If you have no private pension, you can develop a strategy of accumulating RRSP funds so that both you and your spouse qualify for the $1,000 RRSP income exemption.

If you have an RRSP, and if you and/or your spouse are age 65 or over, and you have no private-pension income, then it is to your advantage to use part of the proceeds to purchase the tax-free $1,000 of maturity income. Every year that passes beyond age 65 — in which you have RRSP funds available and you are not using the $1,000 pension/RRSP income exemption — you are missing an opportunity to save money on taxes. If your income is in excess of your immediate needs, you may be reluctant to use part of your RRSP funds to produce more income. However, you can offset the $1,000 increase in income by making a new contribution from earned income, or roll over $1,000 of your Canada Pension into your RRSP. The $1,000 Canada Pension would normally be taxable, and by putting it into your plan you would be saving the tax it would otherwise attract. This would have the effect of increasing the value of your RRSP accounts and replacing the funds used to purchase the $1,000 maturity income in the first place. You can even make a spousal contribution if you are over 71, provided your spouse has not reached age 71. This includes the taxation year of your spouse's 71st birthday, provided the contribution is made before December 31 of that year.

So far, we have said that withdrawals from spousal RRSPs will be taxed in the spouse's hands and not in the contributor's. This is true, except when the withdrawal is less than the sum of the contributions made in the year of withdrawal and the contributions made in the preceding two years. In this case, the withdrawal will be taxable in the hands of the contributor. If the withdrawal is greater than the sum of the contributions made in the year of withdrawal and in the preceding two years, then the contributions will be taxable to the contributor.

Finally, a word of warning. Spousal RRSPs were introduced to give non-working spouses a chance to accumulate assets that would produce a source of independent income on retirement. They work in such a way that once the spousal contribution is made, the spouse in effect owns the contributed funds. Spousal RRSPs are therefore not recommended for a couple whose marriage is likely to disintegrate.

Transfer from other companies. If you already have an RRSP, and you plan to make further contributions, then you should first make a point of reviewing your RRSP's past performance. If you are at all dissatisfied with it, remember that you can transfer the proceeds to one of the plans offered by another company. Such transfers can be made tax-free and do not affect the contribution limits outlined above. Generally, the only requirement is your signature on a "transfer authorization letter," which is available at some RRSP issuers' branch offices. There is an exeption for life insurance plans, which normally require a signed "cash surrender value" form and the return of the policy contract. To effect such a transfer, simply take the cash surrender value form and the policy to the new RRSP issuer, sign the transfer letter, and the new issuer will arrange the transfer. But always keep in mind that your RRSP contributions should earn as much money as possible —

and not just this year's contribution, but all the past ones too.

Let's now have a look at the types of plans that are available, so you can decide which one is best for you. First of all, the common element in all plans is that contributions are held in individual RRSP trusts, and the funds must be invested in any one (or any combination) of the following:

1. Money on deposit at a Canadian bank, trust company or credit union.
2. Bonds — federal, provincial or municipal, including public utilities.
3. Corporate bonds of a company whose shares are traded on a Canadian exchange.
4. Mortgages on real property situated in Canada, provided the property is at "arm's length."
5. Guaranteed Investment Certificates (GICs)of a Canadian trust company.
6. Common stock of a company whose shares are traded on a Canadian exchange.
7. Common stock of a company listed on a foreign exchange (up to a maximum of 10% of your plan's assets).
8. Shares or savings plans of a company which, in turn, invests in the above kinds of securities.

Guaranteed principal RRSPs. Banks, trust companies and credit unions offer term-deposit and savings plan RRSPs. The advantage of these is that your principal is guaranteed. The criteria to examine when looking for one of these RRSPs are the same as those for non-RRSP investments. Obviously, the rate is important. And invariably there is a trade-off between the rate and the length of time you are willing to tie up your funds. Traditionally, the longer the time, the higher the rate. Recently, however, interest rates have been so volatile that you can no longer generalize about what you are likely to find. So you have to check out the rates on the very day you make your investment, if you want to be sure of getting the greatest possible return. Your contribution will be insured against default or bankruptcy of the trust company, credit union or bank — up to a limit of $10,000.

Mutual fund RRSPs. Unlike the "in-house" instruments offered by deposit-taking institutions, the mutual funds are segregated into a trusteed pooled-fund arrangement where the sponsor sells units in a portfolio comprising eligible investments for RRSP purposes. The value fluctuates up or down, depending upon the performance of the securities. The yardstick used for grouping funds is usually the type of investment the fund contains. So there are common stock funds, mortgage funds, income funds and variations of all three. Essentially, pooled funds are equity investments. There is no guarantee of the rate of return, or of the value of the units at any given time.

It is difficult to make a meaningful comparison of the performance of investment funds. An individual fund can move up or down in the rankings depending upon the time period being measured. For example, a widely advertised fund called Industrial Growth was ranked first over the ten-year period ending September 1, 1979; over five years ending the same date, it was ranked 23rd; over three years, it was ranked tenth; and over one year it was ranked 56th. Almost every mutual fund has done well during the past two years because Canadian stocks have advanced strongly. However, the nature of mutual funds is such that while it is possible that today's leaders will head the rankings ten years from now, it is by no means certain.

Self-administered RRSPs. Self-administered RRSPs can be arranged through most major trust companies. However, they only make sense if you want to invest in common stocks or mortgages. Your contribution goes into a special self-directed trust and you simply tell your trustee which of the eligible investments you want to purchase. The performance of the fund will, of course, depend on how good you are at picking winners. Generally, self-administered RRSPs are well suited to the person who is confident he can do a good job managing his own funds over the long haul. They are not recommended for new RRSP plan-holders, or for people who worry when the stock market is down.

The minimum administration fees are in the $75-$250 range, which makes it expensive if you have only a small amount in your plan. There is also a high risk factor for mature taxpayers approaching retirement, because if things go wrong, there may not be enough time to make up losses before you need the money or your plan matures.

Life insurance RRSPs. Most life insurance policies that have a cash surrender value (CSV) are eligible investments as an RRSP. The most common types are whole life, limited-payment life and endowment plans. However, because of the heavy front-end loading to pay sales commissions and set-up charges, they are probably the most inappropriate type of plans to purchase. So much so, in fact, that if you have been waiting for the CSV to reach the value of your total premium outlay, you should probably reassess your situation immediately. If you have dependents and need life insurance for protection, it is better to buy term insurance first, then transfer the CSV of the life insurance policy into a legitimate RRSP.

The best type of plan. It is impossible for us to say which is the best type of plan for you, because there are so many individual factors you have to consider — your age, your tax bracket, your family situation, the disposition of the rest of your assets, and (probably the most important consideration of all) the type of investment you are most comfortable with. However, we can break the decision down to four key considerations:

1. Security of principal. Are your funds guaranteed against loss to a degree that you are happy with? Debt obligations such as GICs or term deposits are the investments that give you the greatest security.
2. The rate of return. Are you getting the maximum rate of return, given the degree of principal security you are seeking? The rate of return will have a crucial effect on the size of your RRSP funds when you retire, and this, in turn, will clearly have a crucial effect on the size of the income you can derive from these funds.
3. Flexibility. Can you get at your RRSP funds in an emergency? Can your plan be cashed in without your having to pay a penalty?
4. Front-end loading. Front-end loading to pay sales commissions should be avoided, since any fees paid up front reduce the size of your deposit. This will obviously reduce the rate at which your funds accumulate, so again it will reduce the amount of money you have available when you retire.

RHOSPs: your house is your best piggy bank

Although RRSPs are the most popular of the tax shelters, they are closely followed by Registered Home Ownership Savings Plans (RHOSPs). Recently, there were some changes to the tax rules regarding RHOSPs, but a RHOSP can still be one of the best tax shelters around — even if you have no intention of ever buying a home.

They work like this: If you and your spouse do not own a home, you may make tax-deductible contributions of up to $1,000 per year to a lifetime maximum of $10,000, thereby sheltering other sources of taxable income. As well, earnings in the plan remain exempt from income tax and thus accumulate on a pre-tax basis. Not only will you have more money to invest, but you'll have more money working for you in the plan.

So far, of course, these features are similar to other deferred income plans such as RRSPs. The main difference relates to the tax breaks that arise when a RHOSP is collapsed. These tax breaks can be dramatic. As in the case with RRSPs and other plans, withdrawals from a RHOSP are potentially taxable. But if RHOSP funds are used to purchase an owner-occupied home in Canada within 60 days of the calendar year in which the withdrawal is made, there will be no tax to pay, provided you move in by the purchase deadline. An owner-occupied home, by the way, includes a house, apartment, cottage, condominium, or a share in a co-op housing corporation. It can even be a mobile home or a house-boat, if you plan to live in it year-round.

Alternatively, you can use your withdrawal to purchase an Income Averaging Annuity Contract (IAAC) in the year of withdrawal or up to 60 days thereafter. If you do, you will be able to spread out your tax bill over the term of the IAAC, which can be for up to 15 years, or for life. Putting the proceeds of a RHOSP into an IAAC can be a particularly good move if you have a large RHOSP, because the withdrawal might otherwise propel you into a high tax bracket, especially since you cannot make a partial withdrawal from a RHOSP. On the other hand, if, for whatever reason, you have a low income year, it may be advisable simply to collapse the plan and pay tax, if you do not intend to purchase a home.

You can also reduce your tax bill if you purchase a home in the next three years after the year in which the withdrawal is made. In this case, you may claim an offsetting deduction for funds used to buy an owner-occupied house in the year of the purchase, if you move in within 60 days of the year end. This is not the same as the tax-free withdrawal that we just mentioned: In this case, the proceeds of the RHOSP will be included in your income in the year you collapse the plan, and then a deduction can be claimed in the year you purchase the home. The amount of the deduction will, of course, be limited to the taxable withdrawal from your RHOSP, minus any contribution you have previously made to an IAAC.

You are entitled to make a contribution to a RHOSP provided that:

* You are at least 18 years of age.
* You are a resident in Canada for tax purposes.
* You have never had a RHOSP before.
* Neither you nor your spouse owns real property used as a dwelling (whether occupied by yourself or anyone else) in the year in which the contributions are made.

Many people are confused about these requirements. The fact that you or your spouse *formerly* owned a home does not prevent you from making a contribution. Also, the fine print in the Income Tax Act states that if you own a piece of real estate that is used for any purpose other than a dwelling, you can still make a contribution. For example, you may contribute if you rent an apartment and own a piece of an office building. But if you own a cottage instead, you can't make a contribution. Also, a special rule allows you to make a contribution in the year you purchase a home. So if you contribute to a RHOSP just before you close your deal, you will get a tax deduction, and be able to withdraw the funds tax-free shortly afterward. Finally, it is perfectly acceptable for both spouses to make tax-deductible contributions to a RHOSP, if they otherwise meet the qualifications.

Sometimes, a person can become ineligible to make further contributions to a RHOSP even though he has not purchased a home. Some years ago, for example, many of us were put in this position when the tax rules were changed to preclude further contributions if your spouse owned a home. This will also occur if you inherit a home, or marry someone who owns one. Under these circumstances, people often get the mistaken idea that they must withdraw the funds and pay tax. In fact, there are a number of better alternatives. First, you can simply leave the money where it is and let it accumulate on a pre-tax basis for up to 20 years from the time the RHOSP was established. The money will then become taxable. But in the meantime, you can accumulate a small fortune on a tax-deferred basis. Secondly, you can still take advantage of the tax breaks described above if you purchase an owner-occupied home in the future. Also, you may recommence your contributions in any year that you are once again able to meet all of the qualifications — for example, if you were to sell your present home and move into an apartment.

Deferred Profit Sharing: your boss is happy — so are you

When it comes to tax shelters, most people think of such vehicles as RRSPs, and RHOSPs — the ones we have just discussed. Deferred Profit Sharing Plans (DPSPs) are often overlooked. They can, however, be an effective method of compensation, and tax planning, too, for both an employee and an employer. Before we get into the advantages, let's have a look at a little background.

DPSPs are a special kind of profit-sharing plan in which the employer's contributions are tax-sheltered as long as they remain in the plan. If the employer's profits are high enough, he may contribute up to the *lesser* of 20% of the employee-member's annual salary or $3,500 (minus current service company pension plan contributions, if any). The result is that:

* Amounts contributed may be deductible by the company for tax purposes.
* The employer's contributions are not currently taxed as income to the employee.
* The employer's contributions may accumulate free of tax within the DPSP until they are ultimately distributed to the employee.

The benefits that you would receive as an employee are similar to the ones you would get from a company pension plan. However, the DPSP will offer you some other benefits too. To begin with, a DPSP doesn't lower the amount that you can contribute to an RRSP; in fact, it can raise it. The maximum RRSP contribution you can make, as a member of a company pension plan, is the lesser of $3,500 or 20% of your earned income, minus your contribution to the pension plan. In contrast, as an employee-member of a DPSP, you can contribute up to $5,500 to an RRSP or 20% of your earned income, whichever is less. This is the maximum deductible contribution our tax laws permit (for the purpose of Quebec income taxes, the $5,500 limit is reduced to $3,500 for a DPSP member).

Next, in addition to your employer's contribution to the DPSP, you can, as an employee, contribute up to $5,500 per year of your own money to the DPSP. Although these contributions are not deductible, they accumulate tax-free in the DPSP until the proceeds of such contributions are distributed to you. Only then do you have to pay tax with respect to the income earned by your contribution; the principal amount of the contributions is still received free of tax.

Since none of the earnings go to the government in the meantime, this means (as with the other tax shelters we've discussed) that there will be more money working for you, the contributor, so you will end up a lot better off, even after the final tax bite. Another advantage is that the employer's contribution to a DPSP will usually reach you more quickly than is the case with the company pension plan. Special rules provide that such contributions must pass to you, the employee, no later than five years from the time of contribution or allocation by the employer. Furthermore, a DPSP generally offers you more flexibility than a company pension plan when you ultimately withdraw funds from the plan. This flexibility (including the right to transfer funds received from a DPSP to an RRSP, or to purchase an annuity) may allow you both to reduce the total amount of tax payable in respect of the benefits, and to defer the payment of such taxes even longer.

As for the employer, he, too, will probably find DPSPs more flexible than a company pension plan. To begin with, since DPSP contributions are based on the profitability of the employer, he will not have to make significant contributions when strapped for cash. Also, company pension plans are subject to strict actuarial requirements, so the employer's contributions to these plans are relatively inflexible. But an employer utilizing a DPSP need not guarantee any minimum pension levels.

Another big advantage to the employer is the flexibility of the investments that may be made with funds in the plan. Depending on the earnings history of the company, the DPSP may even be able to invest in the company's own shares, so that the employer is in the enviable position of being able to deduct his contributions to the DPSP while retaining the use of the money contributed. This often requires a bit of fancy legal footwork, but it can be done.

Many employers will balk at the thought of sharing profits with employees. But remember: as an employer, your contribution can be limited to $3,500 or 20% of an employee's salary, whichever is less. Also, if need be, compensating salary adjustments can be made. Furthermore, there is no requirement that all employees be brought in: A DPSP can be set up for a small number of key employees or even a single employee.

The following example may show the importance of these features: Suppose you are a key employee of a small company. Instead of receiving salary that would be taxable in your hands, your company sets up a Deferred Profit Sharing Plan. The DPSP could be confined to you or extended to other company employees, if so desired. Each year the company pays $3,500 into the plan for your benefit, without your having to pay a cent of tax. Also, earnings on these funds accumulate tax-free. Your company then claims a tax deduction for these contributions, which are invested in a wide range of items, including the company's own shares. In effect, then, the company gets a tax deduction without having to part with its money.

If this process continues for 25 years, assuming a 10% return, the contributions will accumulate to almost $380,000. This compares, for example, with about $88,000, if you were to be paid a salary instead (assuming you are in a 50% tax bracket). Although the $380,000 would be taxable when withdrawn from the plan, there are a number of ways in which you can defer taxes on the accumulated contributions. What's more, if you reach retirement age by the time the contributions are withdrawn, you will probably find yourself in a low tax bracket, so that the tax bite on the $380,000 will be relatively modest.

Besides your company's DPSP contributions on your behalf, you are free each year to contribute to your own RRSP to the maximum limits permissible — the lesser of $5,500 or 20% of earned income. Finally, you can also contribute up to $5,500 per year of your own funds to the DPSP. Although these contributions are not tax-deductible, earnings will accumulate tax-free as long as the contributions remain in the plan. Assuming a 10% rate of return, at the end of 25 years you will find that your accumulated investment will be more than two times greater than would have been the case had you simply invested the money personally.

Fortunately, DPSPs are relatively easy to set up. Often they are established through programs offered by financial institutions such as banks, insurance companies, and trust companies. However, there may be sound financial reasons for going it alone; that is, setting up your own plan. For example, instead of using a trust company, you may select any three adults you choose to administer the plan, as long as at least one of them is independent of the company. In this way, you can eliminate many of the administration fees and commissions that these institutions charge, and put 100% of the contributions into the DPSP to work for you. Also, as you will not be tied down to the standard documentation of an established financial institution, you may set up a plan that is more responsive to the needs of your company. Finally, you will avoid certain restrictions on the investments that most financial institutions impose.

Beware the Vamps: so you want to get into the movies...?

In 1977, approximately $6.5 million was spent in Canada on feature film production; in 1978 the amount rose to $65 million and in 1979 it soared to $150 million. This growth industry has justifiably earned Canada the title "Hollywood North." So what happened to produce such a boom? Federal government rules offer lucrative tax deferrals if you invest in Canadian movies. There are, however, two aspects of investment in Canadian film production that you should consider. The tax deferral is one, of course. The other is the prospect of the film itself, not only to return your capital but also to make you a profit.

Let's look first at the deferral. As a Canadian resident, you are allowed to claim against other income 100% of the production cost of a film that received a certification from the Secretary of State showing it to be a "certified feature production." To qualify for this certification, the film must be not less than 75 minutes in running time; have a Canadian producer; and earn at least six units out of a possible ten for having Canadians as director, screenwriter, actors, art director, photographer, and so on. Also, at least 75% of the service costs must be paid to Canadians, and 75% of the costs of processing and final preparation must be incurred in Canada.

Let's see how you, as a resident of, say, British Columbia, with a taxable income of $55,000, would have fared through the purchase of a $5,000 feature film unit in 1979: Your taxable income would have been reduced from $55,000 to $50,000. The tax that would have been payable on your $5,000 investment at a rate of 52.6% equals $2,630. So your actual capital at risk is $5,000 - $2,630 = $2,370. So, for the unit of $5,000, you put up $2,370, the government of Canada puts up $1,800 and the government of B.C. puts up $930.

You are now partners in a film (which means that, if the film succeeds, your partners get their proportionate shares). Also, you have found a way of getting your two partners to put up their cash first and let you defer paying your share, except out of profits. One recent film offering, for example, allowed you to pay 20% of the unit cost, or $1,000, in cash, and sign a promissory note of $4,000 to mature December 31, 1983 at an annual rate of interest 1% above prime, with interest payable June 30 and December 31. This note must be backed by an irrevocable letter of credit from your bank. This will probably cost you an additional 1% of the face value of the note. As revenues accrue to the custodian of the film, your share would be applied to pay down your note.

How would you make out with this arrangement:

Cost of unit for tax purposes:	$5,000
Tax reduction at 52.6%:	$2,630
Cash paid for unit:	$1,000
Cash flow:	$1,630

Interest cost at, say, 16% on $4,000	
promissory note June 30, 1980:	$320
December 31, 1980:	320
Letter of credit:	40
Total cost:	$680

As this is a tax-deductible expense, tax saved on interest: $680 x 0.526 = $358. Out-of-pocket cost of note: $680 - $358 = $322 (your partners are again picking up their share). Net cash-in pocket after expenses at end of 1980: $1,630 - $322 = $1,308. Of course, we can also assume you would invest your cash-in-pocket and make further income to reduce your $2,370 risk.

Say in 1981 revenues accrue to your film. They will pay down your promissory note. You have to add them to your 1981 taxable income and pay tax out of other cash sources. But remember, you still have an investment regardless of the tax deferral and cash flow, and this is the most important consideration. You should not make an investment simply because of the tax benefits.

So let's now look at what you should consider when assessing the merits of a film. First and probably most important to its commercial, as well as artistic, success are the people and the script. The producer, who has to be a Canadian, should have a track record showing experience in producing films on time and within budget. The stars, who should be attractive, appropriate and, let's hope, box office draws, don't have to be Canadian, but they must appeal to the public. The director should have had previous successes, and so should the scriptwriter.

The next consideration is the budget. Obviously the less the film costs, the less revenue it has to generate to reach the break-even point. The budget should be realistic for the film and, as a general rule, no more than

$4-$5 million. A custodian should hold the funds and only pay accounts after the auditors have approved and verified the expense. The film must also carry a completion guarantee that is provided by a recognized company specializing in such guarantees — for example, Film Finances Ltd. of London, England. The guarantee ensures the film will be completed if it goes over budget or experiences problem in production, so that the unit holders will not be called upon to furnish additional capital.

You should also determine who puts up the balance of the capital if the public subscribers fall short. And examine the contracts, if any, that the producer has made for revenue from the following sources:

* Theatrical distribution — North American and foreign;
* U.S. network television;
* Pay TV;
* Syndicated television.

It is impossible to predict what revenues will accrue from these sources, but obviously the more successful a film is at the box office in North America, the greater will be the price paid by, say, NBC for its "movie of the week." The confidence of the producer in his product can be measured by how many of the revenue sources are pre-sold and for what price. If he doesn't pre-sell anything, he may believe he has a great "box-office" movie.

This is where the budget is important. It is estimated that a movie has to earn four to six times the budget at the box office in North America to recover production costs. *Meatballs* cost approximately $1.6 million; box office is estimated at $60 - $80 million for a tremendous return to the investors. But *Apocalypse Now* cost close to $40 million and although it is drawing well, it will be years before it breaks even. However, it is generally accepted that any reasonable feature film can recover its production costs by the sale of all revenue sources except North American theatrical.

Revenues normally start to flow within 12 months of the completion of principal photography. So if you bought your unit in December, 1980, you should expect a revenue flow before the end of 1981. A feature film earns the major portion of its income two and a half to three years after completion of principal photography. As a guideline you should expect to have your unit cost returned in eighteen months or less. To further protect yourself you should check that revenue from distribution accrues to a custodian, such as a trust company, and that the payout of these revenues comes in a fixed priority:

1. 100% of the unit holders' cost returned to investors.
2. Return of any advances that completion guarantor had made.
3. A bonus to unit holders representing a return on their capital while being used — say, 15%.
4. A 50-50 split between unit holders and the producer, with the producer's share covering any bonus participations to stars, director, and so on.

There are many other factors to consider, so consult your broker or tax consultant. But remember, you must like the film as an investment and not just as a tax shelter. Unfortunately, this simple test rules out most Canadian films as a sensible investment.

Personal Incorporation: is it time you stopped being a person?

Earlier, we said that some types of income are taxed more favorably than others. True enough. But it is also true that the *same* type of income will be taxed more favorably, depending upon who receives it. For example, corporations are sometimes taxed more favorably than are individuals earning the same types of income. As a result, you can often save yourself a lot of tax by turning yourself into a corporation.

Although you stand to gain most by incorporating if you run a small business, you can also benefit if you are in the service sector, working as a salesman, consultant or insurance agent, for example; or if you are a professional, such as a doctor, lawyer or dentist; or if you are self-employed in just about any capacity; or if you have a substantial income that comes from your investments. Let's have a look at each of the groups that can benefit and see how different types of corporations can lead to substantial tax savings.

Small business. Although corporate tax rates in Canada hover around 50%, most small businesses are eligible for a 21% small-business tax deduction at the federal level, as well as further reductions in certain provinces. As a result, combined federal and provincial tax rates for most small businesses are about 25%. If you have any significant taxable income at all, you will, therefore, find yourself in a higher tax bracket than a small business. For example, if you are an Ontario resident with a taxable income of just $3,000, you will be in a higher tax bracket. And if you earn, say, $50,000 from your business and you have $6,000 or so in personal exemptions and other deductions, you should be able to save almost $4,500 per year by incorporating. In other words, you will be able to cut your tax bill by 25%.

So how do you qualify for the small-business tax deduction? The answer depends on which of the following types of business income your company has:

Investment-type businesses. Businesses whose principal purpose is to gain income from investments in property including real estate, mortgages, and so on, will be denied the small-business tax deduction unless:

* The company is in the business of leasing property other than real property; or
* The company has at least six full-time employees, not counting major shareholders. Basically, a person who holds 10% or more of a class of the company's stock, and any one of his relatives, is considered to be a major shareholder. Holdings of persons who do not deal at arm's length will be included in calculating the 10% figure.

Although these two types of businesses will be eligible for the full 21% tax deduction, most investment-type corporations will not be eligible. Even so, there are still a number of tax advantages to maintaining a corporation in this case. For example:

* Persons in tax brackets that exceed corporate tax rates (50% or so, depending on the province) will be able to defer some tax by holding their investments in a corporation;
* When an investment-type corporation pays out dividends, some of the tax previously paid on investment income is refundable. Although the refund is designed so that combined corporate and personal tax on the dividend will approximate the tax payable had the investments not been held by a corporation, there will be a slight tax advantage compared with holding such investments personally.

For example, a top bracket Ontario shareholder will be able to increase his after-pay income by about 7% in this manner;

* The use of a corporation will often facilitate various tax-planning opportunities.

Service and management businesses. These businesses will be eligible for a deduction from federal tax of 12⅔% — as opposed to the full 21% deduction. To be more specific, the following types of businesses will receive the 12⅔% deduction:

* Incorporated professional practices of accountants, dentists, lawyers, medical doctors, veterinarians, and chiropractors;
* A business that provides services where more than two-thirds of its gross revenue from services is derived from one entity and the services can be attributed to major shareholders (see above), unless the company has six or more full-time employees;
* So-called "management" corporations — corporations that provide management services to businesses that are connected with the company.

Service corporations that are not included above — for example, incorporated engineers or architects, or companies that derive two-thirds or less of their gross revenue from a single source — will be eligible for the full 21% small-business deduction. The incorporation of service or management companies will result in tax deferral for persons whose marginal tax rates exceed the combined federal and provincial corporate rates. An Ontario taxpayer with 1979 taxable income of about $15,000 or more will be in a higher tax bracket than would be applicable to a corporation eligible for the 12⅔% federal tax deduction (assuming 10% provincial tax).

The higher your income, the greater the benefits of deferral will be. Let's take an Ontario taxpayer with

$60,000 in taxable income. Without the benefit of a corporation, his 1979 tax bill would be about $25,000. Suppose he incorporated and paid himself salary so that his personal taxable income was $15,000. In this case, combined personal and corporate taxes would be $19,000. In other words, more than $6,000 in taxes would be deferred — more than 17% of his after-tax income without the benefit of a corporation.

When corporate profits of a management or service corporation are paid out to the shareholder via a dividend, the overall tax is designed to approximate that which would be applicable had the income been received personally. However, the net effect may be slightly more (or less) favorable, depending on how low the provincial corporate tax rate is.

As well, there may be an additional silver lining in new rules for management and service corporations: As many people are aware, corporations have been subject to attack by Revenue Canada because they were looked on as attempts to abuse the small business tax deduction. With the new rules in effect, it is likely that the tax people will begin to back off. But a full-scale retreat may not be sounded if it becomes apparent that the new legislation is being abused. One particularly sensitive area could be an incorporated executive who, in reality, functions as an employee.

Active businesses. Businesses other than those described above will qualify for the 21% small-businesses tax deduction on income earned in Canada. They will continue to get the lucrative tax breaks that we described at the beginning of this article.

Now that we've summarized the ground rules, it's time for some specific suggestions:

* If a lot of money is involved, it may still be worth your while to incorporate your investment operations.

* Higher income professionals and persons in the service sector should seriously consider incorporating service or management companies.
* If you have a business that qualifies for the full 21% federal tax deduction, we recommend that you consider incorporating, if your business income is at least $20,000 or so. Below this point, the legal and administrative costs of incorporating will probably outweigh the tax advantages.

For those persons who have already incorporated, we also have some suggestions:

* In some instances, where large scale investment-type operations have been carried on through a variety of corporations or other business organizations, it may be possible to combine the activities into a single corporation having six or more full-time employees so that the 21% federal tax deduction can be obtained.
* Corporations continue to be eligible for the small-business tax deduction until the "cumulative deduction account" (essentially the accumulated pre-tax business profits that have been retained in the corporation) reaches $750,000. However, in the taxation year when the new legislation first applies to the corporation, the cumulative deduction accounts of service and management corporations will be increased by 12.5%. This increase will also occur in any year a corporation carries on management or service activities, but did not do so in the previous year. If it becomes apparent that this increase will take your company over the $750,000 limit, it may be a good idea to pay dividends out of the corporation. It may also be possible to eliminate part or all of the increase by the use of a holding company. See your tax adviser.
* If in a taxation year, a corporation carries on

service or management functions — as well as having income that would otherwise qualify for the full 21% small-business tax deduction — such income will be eligible only for the 12⅔% tax deduction. Therefore, it is a good idea to separate those activities that qualify for the full deduction before the taxation year in which the new rules come into effect.

* Until the tax year when new provisions apply to the company, the old rules allowing a 21% small-business deduction for active business income will continue to be in effect. Therefore, corporations, which will lose part or all of their small business deductions when the new rules come into effect, should consider taking steps to maximize taxable income now so that more income will be taxable at the low rate. This can be done, for example, by *not* claiming reserves, and capital cost allowance, or by deferring expenses.

Top-hat Pensions: why is the boss smiling?

In the spring of 1980, a dramatic tax-saving opportunity opened up for business owners and executives when Revenue Canada changed its stance on so-called "top-hat" pension plans. This opportunity is still not widely known. But the savings can amount to many thousands of dollars, so if you are an executive and/or a business owner, we strongly urge you to study this discussion — and then consult your tax adviser for further details.

First of all, a top-hat pension typically involves a plan that is set up for the exclusive benefit of the owner-managers of a company. The idea is that the company will make large tax-deductible contributions to fund the pension plan, in respect to the owner-managers' services rendered to the company in *previous* years as well as in the current year. Pension benefits would be payable — and taxable — to the owner-managers after retirement, when their marginal tax rates may well be lower. The net effect is that the company obtains immediate and massive tax relief, especially from the past service contributions to the plan, while the owner-managers, in effect, retain the funds.

Until recently, there were stringent rules to ward off this situation. They were aimed at employees who also had a major stake in the company's equity. But in a surprising move, Revenue Canada has now abandoned most of these requirements. As a result, an organization may now set up a pension plan primarily for the benefit of significant shareholders, and make tax-deductible contributions for both past and present services. If a shareholder has been with the company a number of years, the size of the tax-deductible past service contribution can be very large indeed. Consider, for example, the following table. It shows examples of the maximum tax-deductible contributions for past services that can be used to fund a pension payable to a male at age 65 for life, with a guaranteed term of ten years.

		Years of past service	
Age of Employee	**15 years Tax deductible single payment**	**25 years Tax deductible single payment**	**35 years Tax deductible single payment**
40	$ 60,588		
50	$108,504	$180,841	
60	$194,315	$325,858	$453,210
65	$260,037	$433,395	$606,500
Annual pension generated by payment:	$25,725	$42,875	$60,000

Notes:

1. Maximum annual pension benefit is the lesser of:
   (a) 2% of the average of the best three consecutive years of earnings for each year of service (not exceeding 35 years); and
   (b) $1,750 times the number of years of service (not in excess of 35 years).
2. If the company does not have the resources to make the maximum lump-sum contribution, the plan can be designed so that lesser amounts could be contributed until more funds are available, or the funding (and tax deductions) can occur over a number of years.

Now let's look at an example. Suppose you and your business partner are both 60 years of age. You are co-owners of a small electrical contracting company, which you founded 35 years ago, and which your partner joined 25 years ago. Your company could now set up a pension plan exclusively for you and your partner. As can be seen from the table above, assuming that you both qualify for the maximum annual pension, your company could make tax-deductible past service contributions on behalf of the two of you, which would add up to about $932,000. Your company would obtain nearly $1 million in tax deductions from this manoeuvre, but you would not have to pay tax on the contributions until you actually received funds out of the pension plan itself.

As you can see, the tax benefits of a top-hat pension plan can be very dramatic when sizable past service contributions are involved. There is, however, one restriction relating to past service contributions that should be mentioned. Employees who hold at least 10% of the voting shares of a company (this figure includes shareholdings of the immediate family) cannot be eligible for past service contributions in years when the 10%-or-more holding was present, and, in addition, when the employee was a member either of another registered pension plan or a Deferred Profit Sharing Plan of the participating company or a related company.

But there are exceptions even to this restriction, if all funds from such plans are transferred to the new registered pension plan and treated as an employee-required contribution. For the years in which this is done, past service contributions can be made in the new pension plan, if excess funding is required over and above the amounts transferred into the new plan.

Employees' contributions to a pension plan should not be overlooked either. If the plan permits, an employee can make tax-deductible contributions of up to $3,500 per year for current service. In addition to this, deductible past service contributions of another $3,500 per year can be made for years in which the employee did not contribute to the pension plan (for Quebec provincial income tax, the past and current service contribution limits are each $5,500). All told, then, employees can contribute up to $7,000 per year, in addition to the company's contribution to the plan. And like employer contributions, earnings will accumulate tax-free within the plan.

The Year-end: crucial steps for a crucial time

Tax planning is something you should practise all year round but the last six weeks of the year are probably the most important time of all. As a result, we have prepared a list of easy-to-follow, year-end tax-planning ideas. Check through to see if any of the strategies apply to you.

1. Tax-loss selling.

* Whether to sell marketable securities or other capital assets at a loss is more an investment decision than a

tax planning one. But a sale before year-end will give you tax relief one year earlier.

* As we've indicated before, capital losses are fully deductible against capital gains (one-half of any remainder is taxable). If losses exceed gains, you may deduct one-half of excess capital losses against other sources of income, to a maximum of $2,000. Excess losses can be applied to last year's tax return and carried forward to future years in a similar manner. Note: In most cases, losses from personal-use property are non-deductible.
* Shares should be sold at least five business days before the year-end to get losses into that year.
* If you own assets that are practically worthless, a sale at fair market value (usually nominal) or a gift to a friend or relative will result in a loss, unless transfer is to your spouse, a corporation controlled by you or your spouse, or your own or your spouse's RRSP. Make sure you document the transfer carefully.
* If you purchase an identical property within 30 days before or after the sale of a loss item, your capital loss will be disallowed. This also applies if your spouse or a controlled corporation purchases identical property. So, if you bought shares in 1975, say, for $2,000 and wished to sell them in late December, 1980 for $500, your capital loss would be disallowed if either you or your spouse repurchased the stock within 30 days of the sale.
* Losses from bad debts for income-earning purposes can be deducted without an actual sale. And so can losses on shares of bankrupt companies.

2. Tax-gain selling. Sometimes it is a good idea to trigger a capital gain before the end of the year.

* Taxable capital gains from the sale of most Canadian securities are eligible for the Canadian investment income deduction of $1,000. If you have not fully utilized this deduction, consider selling before year-end to get a

tax-free gain. The security can be re-acquired early in the new year, if you wish.

* If you are in a lower tax bracket this year than next, you'll pay less tax on gains incurred before the end of the year.
* The first $200 of capital gains from the appreciation of a foreign currency are tax-exempt. Consider converting part of a foreign currency bank account for a tax-free gain and reinvesting early in the new year.
* If part of the proceeds on a sale are not due until next year, you can generally offset part or all of your capital gain by a reserve. In the case of a capital gain, the deduction allowed is generally:

$$\frac{\text{amounts due after end of year}}{\text{total proceeds}} \times \text{taxable capital gain}$$

Thus, if you sold an asset at the end of 1980, but the proceeds were not receivable until 1981, the entire 1980 gain could be offset by a reserve.

* Alternatively, a tax on a 1980 gain can be spread over a number of years if you purchase an Income Averaging Annuity Contract within 60 days after the year-end.

3. Deductible payments. Make payments that are tax-deductible before the end of the year to get tax deductions in that year. Here are a few:

* Charitable donations. If the total of your charitable donations and allowable medical expenses (i.e. deductible medical bills in excess of 3% of your net income for tax purposes) is under $100, you can claim a $100 optional standard deduction instead. Consider making 1981 charitable donations before the end of 1980 in order to exceed the $100 threshold in 1980. Then, in 1981, claim the $100 optional standard deduction. For example, if you make a $90 donation every January, make your 1981 donation before the end of 1980, so

that 1980 charitables will total $180. In 1980 you will get the $180 deduction, and in 1981 you can claim the $100 optional deduction.

Generally, you can't deduct charitable donations in excess of 20% of "net income for tax purposes" (i.e. income before personal exemptions, and so on. But excess deductions can be carried forward one year, subject to the same 20% limitation. Exceptions to this rule include gifts to federal or provincial governments, and a gift of Canadian cultural property to certain institutions, if it is certified to meet the criteria of the Canadian Cultural Property Export and Import Act.

* Political donations. The federal government allows a tax *credit* for contributions made before the end of the year to registered political parties or candidates in a federal general election or a by-election. For the first $100 you contribute, 75% of the contribution will be available as a credit. For contributions between $100 and $550, you will get $75 plus 50% of the excess of your contributions over $100. For contributions between $550 and $1,150, you will get $300 plus one-third of the excess over $550. For contributions in excess of $1,150 no further credit is available. Ontario, Alberta and Quebec give credits from provincial taxes for donations made to provincial political parties, and similar organizations.
* Moving expenses. If you have stopped working in one place, and moved elsewhere in Canada, you may claim certain moving expenses, provided that the move brings you at least 25 miles closer to your new place of work. This is the case even if you remain with the same firm. Special rules apply to students and those who are deemed (for tax purposes) to be Canadian residents. Further information on this topic can be obtained in the booklet *Moving Expenses*, available free of charge from your District Taxation Office.

* Tuition fees. Only a student can deduct them, even if you pay the fees on his or her behalf. But if the student has income, taking a deduction will increase your ability to claim the student as a dependent, since this claim is based on the student's net income. If you send your child to a school in which religion is taught, part (part or all) of the tuition fee is often considered to be a charitable donation. You are allowed to deduct this portion. An often overlooked point is that you can claim tuition fees on either an academic- or calendar-year basis (as long as you don't count the same fee twice). For example, if you pay for the winter term in September, you may either take the deduction that year, or wait until the next. The latter alternative may be desirable if, next year, you expect to find yourself in a higher tax bracket.
* Medical expenses. Medical expenses must exceed 3% of your net income to give you a deduction. Even if they do, there will be no benefit, unless the excess, when added to your charitable donations, totals more than $100, since you can claim a $100 optional standard deduction instead. Medical expenses may be claimed for any 12-month period that ends in the calendar year. It is usually advantageous to take the 12-month period in which the medical expenses are highest, because of the 3% limitation.

Either spouse may claim the other spouse's medical expenses even if the spouse is not claimed as a dependent. It is often a good idea to have the spouse with the lower income claim all the medical expenses, since there will then be more expenses in excess of 3% of net income. As well, you may deduct the medical expenses of any dependent whom you are entitled to claim as an exemption on your return.

* Alimony and maintenance payments. Make sure you comply with all the tax requirements. Details can be

obtained in *Income Tax and the Single Parent,* a booklet available from your District Taxation Office.

Other payments that should be made before year-end to get that year's deductions are:

* Union dues and professional dues;
* Child care expenses (a booklet on the subject is available from your District Taxation Office);
* Investment counsel fees;
* Carrying charges relating to your investment income such as interest paid or safety deposit box charges; (Note: You may also deduct interest expenses as they become payable.)
* Payments to dependent parents, grandparents, siblings, aunts and uncles — in certain instances.

4. Tax shelters.

* The deadline for contributions to a RHOSP Plan is December 31. If you and your spouse do not own a home, you may make tax-deductible contributions of up to $1,000 per year, to a lifetime maximum of $10,000. Earnings in the plan remain exempt from income tax and thus accumulate on a pre-tax basis.
* Consider investing in Canadian films before year-end, but make sure the films are good investments in their own right.
* Deadline for tax-deductible contributions to RRSPs and Income Averaging Annuity Contracts is 60 days after the year-end. But early contributions will result in more earnings accumulating on a tax-deferred basis in the plans.

5. Interest income.

* You have the option of receiving interest income either as it is earned, or when you actually receive cash payments.
* Choosing the "cash method" will often result in a deferral of tax until after the year-end.
* Some securities allow you to control the receipt of

interest — for example, bond with coupon features. If you own such a security that pays interest eligible for the $1,000 Canadian investment income deduction, choosing the cash method allows you to ensure that you receive enough interest to fully utilize the deduction. Also, you may be able to take in income in years when you're in a low tax bracket.

* Sometimes choosing the "earned method" will smooth out interest income — especially when interest is payable in a lump sum. This could help you to fully utilize the Canadian investment income deduction.

Different methods of reporting interest income may be used for different sources of interest income, including different types of obligations issued by the same debtor. But you must be consistent in your method of reporting interest from any single source.

Part 3

REAL ESTATE

Deducting Your Mortgage: yes, you can do it

When the federal Conservative government went down to defeat in the February 18, 1980 general election, one result was the death of its promised across-the-board tax relief for homeowners. However, you may still be able to obtain tax deductions for mortgage interest, and other household expenses, if you have an investment portfolio you are able to fit yourself squarely within certain tax rules. As we mentioned in an earlier discussion, one problem that has vexed taxpayers for years is having non-deductible interest expenses from household or other personal borrowing, while at the same time having unleveraged income-earning investments. Remember, to be deductible, interest and other carrying charges must be incurred to produce taxable income.

In some situations, arranging your affairs to fit within this rule is easy. To use our earlier example, if you intend to buy a color TV as well as some shares, you can obtain deductions for borrowing expenses if you finance the latter and not the former. However, because of the size and repayment restrictions of mortgages, it's easy to fall into the trap of having a big mortgage and an unleveraged investment portfolio, both at the same time. But, even without the Conservatives' mortgage interest and property tax credit proposals, it is still possible to arrange your financial affairs so that you can deduct your mortgage interest. The key, as we said, is to "tie in" your mortgage interest to your income-earning activities.

For example, suppose you have a $100,000 house, and you pay $8,000 a year in interest on a $75,000 mortgage. Suppose, too, that you own an $85,000 investment portfolio, which you purchased for cash. You are then paying too much tax, because your $8,000 interest expense is for personal, not investment, purposes. It is therefore non-deductible. If you wanted to deduct the mortgage interest, you could:

* Sell your investment;
* Use the proceeds to pay off your mortgage;
* Borrow money by re-mortgaging your house to purchase a new investment portfolio.

You could then argue that the purpose of the new mortgage is to purchase an income-earning investment portfolio. Consequently, the mortgage interest is deductible. Of course, this procedure could be complicated by factors such as capital-gains tax on the investment sale, restrictions on paying off the mortgage or difficulty in replacing the investment. But in many instances, this manoeuvre will work.

Investing in an RRSP can be another effective way you may be able to deduct your mortgage interest. Here's what you do:

* Borrow money to contribute to an RRSP — the interest will be deductible as long as the RRSP is in your name;
* Use the tax you save from contributing to the RRSP — and other funds if possible — to pay down your mortgage (not the RRSP loan);
* Later, refinance your mortgage, and then use the proceeds to repay the RRSP loan.

You should now be able to argue that your mortgage interest is deductible, since you have refinanced a debt that was originally incurred to produce income. The same principles can apply when you are about to acquire other income-earning investments. You borrow to purchase your new investment, using the funds that would have been earmaked for the purchase to pay down your mortgage instead; then you refinance your home and pay off the investment loan.

Although these manoeuvres can help you if you now have non-deductible mortgage interest, your best bet is to avoid getting into such a situation in the first place. If you anticipate having large personal expenses that require financing, you are better off borrowing money to purchase your investments and paying your personal expenses in cash. Along the same lines, you may find it worthwhile to use your savings to pay off your mortgage rather than to purchase new investments. Even if the investments yield more than your mortgage interest, the after-tax return may be less than the interest you save by paying off your mortgage.

For example, if you're in a 50% tax bracket, you'll be better off repaying even an 11% mortgage than purchasing a 20% fully taxable investment, since you would net only 10% after tax. If your investment activities are substantial, another way you may be able to claim part of your household expenses is to set aside a portion of your home and use it exclusively for your income-earning activities. You may deduct a portion of general expenses such as:

* Mortgage interest (but not principal),
* Rent,
* Hydro,
* Heat,
* Repairs,
* Insurance,
* Real estate taxes, and so on.

Also, you may deduct specific office expenses, such as supplies and stationery and capital cost allowance on office equipment. (Note: In most cases it is not advisable to claim capital cost allowance on the home itself, since this will jeopardize your home's tax status as a principal residence.) Usually the amount of your deduction may be calculated by pro-rating general expenses on the basis of floor space or number of rooms, and then adding your specific office expenses. While we're on the subject, deductions for an office in the home may also be taken if the office is used for business or professional purposes. In these cases, if it is merely a "second office," you will have to show that it has all the trappings of a *bona fide* office — such as a business telephone listing, appreciable amounts of business being done there, and so on. Employees and commission salesmen may also be eligible to deduct certain expenses for an office in the home. Obtain Interpretation Bulletin IT-352 from your District Taxation Office for details.

Trendy New Mortgages: choosing the best one for you

In the past two years or so, interest rates, and hence mortgage rates, have been fluctuating wildly. The result, at times, has been near-panic among homeowners whose mortgages have come up for renewal during one of the mortgage-rate peaks. Lenders, for their part, have been faced with the same degree of uncertainty. And they have reacted by introducing an array of new mortgage types. Mortgage arrangements now, in fact, are more flexible than they've ever been before. So if you are in the market for a mortgage — either a new one or a renewal of an old one — don't just take the standard five-year-term, 25-year-amortization mortgage. That may be the best one for you, but before you can really be sure that it is, you should first check out the many alternatives.

The major new mortgage products that you should investigate are: graduated payment mortgages (GPMs); the flexible loan insurance program (FLIP); institutionally available open mortgages; and flexible-term mortgages. Most have been introduced only in the past two years.

Flexible term mortgages. These are now available from many institutions for one-to-four-year periods. As in the usual five-year-term mortgage, the lender usually allows you to renew or "roll over" the mortgage loan when it's due. Interest rates on these shorter term loans are usually lower, reducing your monthly payments. Furthermore, if rates go down, you may benefit, while borrowers with five-year-term mortgages continue paying the old higher rates. Of course, if you guess wrong and rates rise, you could be stuck with higher monthly payments much sooner.

In two cases, shorter terms may make sense, whichever way rates go. If you're planning to sell soon, the buyer may not want to assume your mortgage. With a short-term mortgage, you could avoid penalty fees involved in early discharge. A short-term mortgage also makes sense if you're anticipating a windfall profit, say, in a year. You could use the windfall to lower the outstanding principal, thus cutting your monthly payments, and you wouldn't have to pay any penalties to do it. For the same benefit you could also consider an open mortgage.

Open mortgages. These mortgages, generally available in one-to-three-year terms from institutions, and almost always available from private lenders and vendors, allow you to reduce the outstanding principal at no penalty before the term expires. The result is that more of your monthly payment goes toward reducing principal than would otherwise be the case. Rates on open mortgages range from one-quarter to one-half a percent more than on closed mortgages, depending on the lender and whether the loan is NHA-insured or conventional. Despite the higher rate, open mortgages are proving very popular: Some banks are reporting that 26%-27% of their new mortgages are open.

Remember, though, that open mortgages vary among institutions. Some allow prepayments as multiples only of principal and interest; others allow any amount to be prepaid. Still others allow you to repay fixed percentage lump sums of principal once a year. Be sure, too, to check whether the lender requires any other payments (by whatever name they're called) or notification of your intent to prepay.

Graduated payment mortgages. The federal government's National Housing Association-insured GPMs are probably the most controversial of the new mortgages. In a GPM, monthly payments start at a lower level than payment on a standard-level-payment mortgage for the same amount. But the payments increase in later years to reimburse the lender for principal repayment and interest that is *foregone* in the early years. Also, the total loan cost is higher than it is for a level-payment loan.

In effect, a GPM is a "loan within a loan." Its purpose is to allow you to buy a more expensive home than you could otherwise afford. Theoretically, your income will rise with time, so that you will be able to meet the steadily increasing payments. But there are high risks in the NHA-insured GPMs. The graduation is slow, but steady. For example, on a $54,000 mortgage at 13% amortized over 25 years, your payments would rise from $474 a month in the first year of the mortgage to $689 a month in the ninth year, compared with $596 a month with a level-payment mortgage. Can you be sure your income will rise sufficiently to meet those increases, especially as family living and home-maintenance expenses rise? Also, using this same example, you would actually owe *more* than you originally borrowed for nearly 11 years — that is, until you paid off the "loan within a loan" that allows you to graduate your payments. These drawbacks have kept almost all the major lenders away from the program.

Flexible loan insurance program. FLIP mortgages were introduced to Canada in early 1979 by Toronto-based home-builder Victoria Wood, which holds the right to this franchised proprietory mortgage form. The mortgages are now available through more than 50 real estate brokers and builders across Canada. Participating lenders include the Toronto Dominion Bank and three trust companies — Inland, Pioneer and Norfolk.

FLIP mortgages were primarily designed to enable young families earning $20,000-$25,000 a year to afford home ownership. As in the government-insured GPM, your payments on a FLIP mortgage would start off at less than the principal-plus-interest needed to pay off your loan. Gradually, payments rise and level off — typically, after the sixth year — to a somewhat higher level than would be the case with a level-payment mortgage. But, unlike the GPM, the difference between what you are actually paying and what the payment should really be isn't added to your loan. This is because the difference is made up from a "pledged savings account" that you open in conjunction with your down payment. The lender automatically withdraws enough money — savings and earned interest — to make up the difference, gradually reducing the account to zero.

With a FLIP, you create a larger mortgage than you would if the downpayment were made in the usual manner. The benefit is in being able to buy a home with initial lower-than-usual monthly payments, or in buying a more expensive home than your monthly income could otherwise support. Over a 25-year period, a FLIP mortgage costs about 5%-7% more than a traditional mortgage. But not until the 11th year do your interest payments exceed those of a level-payment mortgage.

Other recent changes that may help you in arranging a mortgage include:

* **A higher gross debt ratio.** On both conventional and

NHA-insured loans, most institutions now allow mortgage interest, principal and property taxes to take up 30% of your gross monthly income vs. the previously acceptable 25%. Some eager institutions allow your costs to go as high as 35% of gross income. But unless your other expenses are low, this could be a dangerous concession.

* **Increased NHA lending limits.** These were recently increased to $79,000 anywhere in the country, calculated at 95% of the first $60,000 and 75% of the remainder.

Finally, it always pays to shop around for the best terms. The obvious sources of funds are the banks, trust companies, life insurers and credit unions. When borrowing from a credit union, or taking out a second loan, watch how often interest is compounded; the more frequent the compounding, the higher the effective interest rate. For example, a 12½% mortgage loan compounded monthly carries an effective interest rate of 12.83%. Other sources include mortgage brokers — many of whom no longer charge you a fee — and the person from whom you buy your home. Often, vendors are willing to advance first and/or second mortgages to ensure a sale. Also, private mortgages are typically open and at a lower-than-institutional rate.

Your Principal Residence: making your castle secure

As you no doubt know, the sale of a principal residence is a key exception to the general rule that capital gains are taxable. However, many Canadians pay taxes needlessly because they fail to take full advantage of the principal-residence rules. To begin with, a principal residence is any housing unit owned alone or jointly, which is ordinarily inhabited by a person or a family member (see below) at any time during the year. This includes such property as condominiums, vacation homes, farms, apartments, shares in a housing co-op, or even a residential trailer or houseboat. Any adjoining land that contributes to the use and enjoyment of your home is also subject to the principal-residence rules.But if the land exceeds one acre, you must establish that the excess is necessary for such use and enjoyment. If you can't, you won't qualify for the exemption. (One idea: Show that zoning bylaws require you to have a large lot.)

In most cases, the sale of a principal residence is tax-exempt. But exceptions can occur — for example, when your house has not always been used as your principal residence since you purchased it. Under these circumstances, you calculate your capital gain in the normal manner, but the gain will be reduced by:

$$\text{Capital gain} \times \frac{\text{1 + the number of years after 1971 the house was used and designated as a principal residence (and you were resident in Canada)}}{\text{Number of years of ownership after 1971}}$$

A person can designate only one property as a principal residence for a particular year. But suppose you and your wife each own a home. Both homes could be designated as principal residence — one is yours and one is your wife's. Full exemptions could then be claimed on both, provided that both homes were ordinarily inhabited by their owners, the owner's spouse, a former spouse, or a dependent child at some time during the year, and provided that neither home was principally used to earn income. The dependent child must be under 21, unless mentally or physically infirm, or a fulltime student.

For example, suppose you own a house in Canada in which you and your wife live. Suppose then that you buy a condominium in Florida for vacation purposes and you put it solely in your spouse's name. As long as rental income from the condominium is relatively small, your spouse can claim the condominium as a principal residence, while you can claim the home in Canada as your principal residence. Unfortunately, there is a tendency among couples to own homes in co-tenancy (that is, jointly or otherwise). This may be egalitarian, but it is also bad tax planning when two homes are involved. Although a home in co-tenancy may be designated by either spouse as a principal residence, each spouse must designate his or her interest in order to obtain a full exemption. However, because of the one-principal-residence-per-year, the second home cannot then be designated by a spouse in any year that he or she claims the first home as a principal residence. Thus, if either or both homes are in co-tenancy, you will lose valuable exemptions.

Suppose, for example, that you and your wife own a city home in Toronto and a vacation home in Wasaga Beach, both in joint tenancy. If you sell the city home and wish to eliminate capital gains tax by claiming the principal residence exemption on it, both you and your wife will have to designate your respective interests in the Toronto home. For the years in which this is done, the home in Wasaga Beach cannot be designated as a principal residence, so that capital gains tax will have to be paid when it is sold.

Similarly, if the Toronto home was owned solely by your wife, but the Wasaga Beach property was owned jointly, then your wife could designate the Toronto home. But she would "use up" her exemption, so that only your part of the Wasaga Beach property would be fully exempt. If you're in this situation, we suggest that you convey your homes so that each is wholly owned by one spouse. You will find that this is a relatively simple matter: In most places, no land transfer tax should be involved and legal fees will be modest. The precise tax results of this manoeuvre are sometimes complex. But generally, the effect appears to be as follows:

* **Two homes previously owned in co-tenancy.** Revenue Canada appears to take the position that each spouse will be eligible to claim the principal residence exemption as if he or she had owned the home outright during the years of co-ownership. In other words, the principal residence exemption will be retroactive.
* **One home previously owned in co-tenancy and the second owned outright.** Again, Revenue Canada appears to take the position that the principal residence exemption will be retroactive, so that one spouse can claim the exemption on the co-owned home as if he or she had owned it outright during the years of their co-ownership. The other spouse will be free to claim the second home as a principal residence.
* **Both homes owned in the name of one spouse.** The predominant opinion is that only one home may be claimed as a principal residence during the years when both homes were in the name of one spouse (this is not altogether clear). But both homes can be claimed after the transfer.

Another situation in which a gain may not be fully exempt is when you rent out your home, or otherwise change its use from personal to income-earning purposes. In this case, you may file a letter with your tax return for the year in which the change of use occurs to the effect that you elect (pursuant to subsection 45 (2) of the Income Tax Act) not to have begun to use your residence as an income-producing property. The following are the advantages of doing this:

* Even though you do not actually occupy your home,

you can designate it as a principal residence for up to four years after the change-of-use year. If the change of use arises because an unrelated employer transfers you or your spouse to a new location, you can extend your home's eligibility indefinitely — not just for four years — but you must move at least 25 miles closer to the new location. Also, you must move back during the term of employment. (If the job terminates, you have until the end of the next taxation year to move back.) In either case, you must be a resident in Canada to be able to designate a principal residence. Also, the one-principal-residence-per-year rule applies; so if you move into another home, only one can be designated, although, as before, you can "double up" if the other home is in your spouse's name.

* There are certain tax rules that say you are considered to have "sold to yourself" at market value when you change from personal use to income use, and vice versa. These rules most often have adverse tax results when you move back into the home: Any increase in the home's value during the income-producing years would be taxed. These results will not occur if you file a-change-of-use election. There are some disadvantages to a change-of-use election. Notably, you cannot claim capital-cost allowance (depreciation for tax purposes) on your home during the income-producing period. However, when you move back in, certain rules would probably result in previous years' capital cost allowance being brought back into income anyway. Also, you cannot make an election when changing from producing to personal use. Some tax practitioners advocate buying a rental property and later moving in yourself so that you may tack four years on to the principal residence exemption. Obtain Interpretation Bulletin IT-120R from your District Taxation Office for details. In addition to the subjects

covered here, the Bulletin deals with special rules for farms, as well as partial changes of use, such as renting out part of your home.

Home Improvements: which ones pay off best?

If you own a house, as a principal residence or a rental property, the chances are you have considered making some improvements to it. Also, if you are now thinking of selling that house, you are probably wondering how you can dress it up so that you will be able both to sell it with ease and for as high a price as possible.

In both cases, assuming you don't have unlimited funds, you will be facing a choice. Exactly what improvements should you make, and which ones will give you the highest return? If you have $10,000, say, or maybe $15,000 to spend, how can you best allocate that money? Should you revamp the bathroom by adding new fixtures, add a new garage, sandblast the exterior, or put in a vaulted ceiling upstairs? One of these choices will increase the market value of your house — and its salability — much more than the others. But which one is it? Bear in mind, too, that increased salability and increased market value don't always go hand in hand. Increased market value *usually* spells increased salability. But something that increases salability won't necessarily reap you a higher price when you sell. So how do you determine which changes to make to increase salability and/or market value?

Upgrading With An Eye To Value*

	Improving salability			Improving market value**		
	greatly/	somewhat/	not at all/	more/	same/	less/
Adding a rec. room	39%	42%	10%	17%	48%	21%
Improved bathrooms	52%	29%	10%	55%	24%	6%
Renovating kitchen	66%	23%	3%	42%	31%	13%
Broadloom	38%	45%	17%	10%	35%	45%
Installing a sauna	3%	34%	55%	3%	14%	65%
Central air-conditioning	45%	35%	14%	19%	52%	21%
Window air-conditioning	0%	26%	61%	0%	16%	68%
Adding a sunporch	21%	58%	21%	7%	23%	55%
Fencing a backyard	31%	55%	17%	7%	41%	31%
Fencing front yard	0%	34%	48%	3%	17%	52%
Storage huts	3%	17%	59%	3%	10%	59%
Brick or stone wood-burning fireplace	74%	19%	3%	38%	45%	12%
Extra washroom	45%	35%	7%	29%	52%	14%
In-ground pool	3%	31%	48%	0%	24%	69%
Above-ground pool	7%	7%	72%	0%	3%	83%
Adding a garage	52%	24%	3%	48%	34%	10%

* Some answers don't add to 100%.

** In relation to the cost of the renovation.

Courtesy Toronto Real Estate Board

The Toronto Real Estate Board recently surveyed 101 of its member brokers for their views on the specific effects of different renovations. We've reprinted some of the responses above. The table shows just how real estate agents, who are in the market everyday, *think* the salability and market value of your house will be affected by various renovations. For example, it shows that 39% of the agents polled think that adding a recreation room to your home will "greatly" improve its salability, and another 42% think it will "somewhat" improve the salability. However, only 17% of the agents think that adding a recreation room will increase the value of the house by more than the cost of adding the rec room. Fully 69% feel that you will either just earn your investment back when you sell the house, or else come out with an actual loss. Adding a new rec room, therefore, might be a good idea if you think your house's salability is poor, but it's not such a good idea if you are hoping to make a quick profit on a renovation investment.

Although this survey is helpful, you shouldn't take it as gospel. Like any survey, it's only an indication of general views. Conclusions that apply in one house in one area may be all wrong for another, because each house is unique. Even in a row of look-alike homes, each differs. And the longer the homes are occupied, the more they differ, as succeeding owners modify them.

Nevertheless, some guidelines are universal. The first general rule applies to location. A poor location can erase the value of nearly every improvement. So if your house is badly situated, you probably won't profit, no matter what renovation investment you make. One renovator we know spent $25,000 gutting and rebuilding a run-down inner-city home. Normally, that's a splendid idea. But the house happens to be on one of the busiest north-south streets in the city — and the only renovation for several miles in either direction. After six months, the renovator's ads have taken on a distinctly desperate tone. He will almost certainly lose money.

A second general rule is that you should avoid renovations that make your house the most expensive one in your area. You may enjoy the added features. But the price you get when you sell will likely be dragged down by the neighborhood; it won't reflect your investment. Of course, your improvements might spark imitators. But that could take years. So unless you're prepared to wait, it's probably safer to be a follower than a pioneer.

So how about specifics? Most major renovations are now taking place in the downtown sections of big cities. So in those areas, these are the renovations you should consider first.

* **Modernized and additional bathrooms.** You don't have to go to the extremes of one wealthy matron whose home features several bathrooms nearly 20 feet

square, with gold fixtures, antique furnishings and artwork. But if you improve your existing bathroom, or add a second one, you should be making a wise investment.

* **Modernized kitchens,** with cabinet-and counter-space sufficient to contain all the paraphernalia of North American cooking, are also good ways to boost market value and salability.
* **Openness and light** get top billing from brokers and professional renovators. Skylights, sliding patio doors, enlarged windows, all increase salability enormously. "We get as much space as possible out of a home," stresses one successful renovator, whose sole business is buying, then gutting, rebuilding and reselling downtown homes. He opens up to the rafters and down to the basements. Some of his designs include three-storey atriums. Radicalism in the pursuit of openness can pay big returns, he says.
* **Fireplaces** get top marks, too, in increasing salability. Those in older homes may have to be rebuilt and the hearths enlarged. Check carefully for "hidden" fireplaces in your own home. In many older homes, original fireplaces have been covered over by later generations who considered them "old-fashioned" and unsightly.
* **Opening up unused attic space** to create either a third floor, loft-type study, or simply a high-ceilinged second floor.
* **Provision for parking.** Suburbanites may find it strange, but many downtown homes have no parking. If that's the case, you should add either a basement garage or pave your front yard for parking. You'll need city, and usually neighbor, approval to do so. But it's an improvement that shouldn't be passed up. It can add thousands of dollars to the price you get for your house, and easily make the difference between a sale and a

no-sale. However, adding a garage to a downtown house that already has parking space probably won't do anything but set you back the cost of the garage.

* **An extra bedroom,** particularly in a two-bedroom home, may increase salability. But it may not raise the market value more than the cost of building it in the first place.

On other improvements, opinion is more divided. Some professional renovators routinely lower basements in order to build recreation rooms. Yet brokers are generally skeptical of their value. "Many of them are done poorly and they're too low," complains one broker. "As a buyer, I would probably prefer to put one in myself." Central air-conditioning is a great sales tool in July and August, but otherwise is little appreciated. In-ground swimming pools fall into the same doubtful category. You may decide to put one in for your personal enjoyment. But many buyers will see your pool only as a costly nuisance, robbing them of their backyard and peace of mind. Don't be surprised if they fill it in. Finally, concentrate your renovation money on the *interior* rather than the exterior. That's where families live. A neat, clean exterior appearance is sufficient. In fact, a growing trend in inner city areas is to present an anonymous face to the world. That way you avoid attracting the attention of burglars.

Selling Your Home: how to do it yourself

If you are planning to sell your home, you obviously want to get as high a price as possible for it — or, more accurately, you want to get as much money left in your hand, after the sale has been completed. One of the best ways you can do this is to sell your home yourself without the services of a real estate agent. More work will be involved for you, since you will have to take on the tasks your agent would normally do. But the potential savings are so high that you will easily be compensated for the additional effort.

As you probably know, real estate agents work for the vendor, not for the buyer. So it is you, the seller, who pays the agent his fees. These fees usually amount to 5%-6% of the sale price of the home. And since the average house price in Canada is now more than $65,000, this means you would likely be paying an agent a fee of between $3,000 and $4,000. By selling your own home, you may not be able to receive all this money as a saving: The buyer of your home, knowing that you are bypassing an agent, will expect to pay a lower price. Even so, you should be able to pocket at least $2,500. So how do you go about selling your own home?

First, you should not try to do everything yourself. That means, specifically, that you should engage a lawyer right from the start. Tell him exactly what you are planning to do, and make sure that he is able to help you with the legal and financial aspects of the sale. You would likely use a lawyer anyway, whether you hired a real estate agent or not, so his fees will not be an additional cost. Also, unlike a real estate agent, a lawyer has skills and an expertise that you cannot acquire in the time it would take to sell your home. So lawyer's fees are a worthwhile investment.

The second thing you should do is get your house ready for sale. This, of course, is something you should do, even if you are using an agent. Remember that first impressions are extremely important, so make sure that the outside of your house and your front yard — the parts that potential buyers will see first — are clean and tidy. Lawns should be cut, shrubbery trimmed, and sidewalks and paths swept and cleared. Also, if there is any paint peeling from the outside of your house, this should be touched up or even redone.

Inside, you should also clean thoroughly. Potential buyers will not be like guests to your home; they will poke and prod into every corner and behind every immovable object, so a superficial sweeping of dust under the rug will not be enough. Don't forget to clean out the garage and the basement. Throw away any old junk that you have collected over the years, and stack whatever is left as compactly as possible. Large, open spaces make garages and basements (and rooms and closets, too, for that matter) seem much larger than they really are. If you decide you have to redecorate before you sell, make sure you choose neutral colors (garish reds and deep purples may suit your taste, but they turn most people away). Also, make sure that any redecoration is in keeping with your home's setting, its age and its layout.

Perhaps most important of all, make sure that everything in your house is working as it should. Lights, electrical outlets, taps (no leaks), furnaces, humidifiers, and so on, should all be functioning. The buyer is certain to test them, and nothing kills a sale quite as rapidly as a back-flooding toilet. Also, if your prospective buyer finds something isn't working, he will mentally start lowering his offering price. You should also fill up any cracks in the plaster — walls as well as ceilings — and paint them over. Remember, too, that two other most common reasons for a lost sale are signs of dampness on the ceiling immediately under the roof, and on the walls or the floor of the basement. Again, make repairs and paint over the evidence.

Your next step is to decide how much money you should ask for your house. Your most obvious course of action here is to check out the prices of homes that recently sold in your neighborhood, choosing ones that are similar in size, features and setting as yours. There will almost certainly be some houses in your area that are still on the market. Go and look at these, both inside and out, and compare them in detail with your own home; then set your price in relation to theirs. If you've got a little nerve, you can get a number of real estate agents around to your house and ask them to price it for you. They, in the belief that they will get your business, will be happy to oblige. Most likely, though, the agents will quote a figure that is slightly high, since they will want to impress you with their ability to fetch a good price. But by combining their estimates with your own observations, plus checking out the Multiple Listing Service listings and newspaper ads, you should be able to reach an accurate figure.

Two points are worth bearing in mind here. First, be realistic in setting your price — you'll never make a sale if you ask too much. At the same time, though, always ask for more than you expect or want to get. That way, you'll have some bargaining room when it comes time to haggle with the buyer. Also, if you want to get $80,000 and you ask for $87,000, you might end up with $82,000. It's worth a try. As a final resort, if you still don't trust your own judgment, you can get a professional appraiser to put a price on your house for you.

Your next step is to attract serious, potential buyers.

That's pretty easy to do, since would-be buyers of houses will be out roaming the streets, actively seeking a likely buy. You don't have to entice them out with a clever "come-on." Put a large "for sale" sign on your front lawn, indicating that it's a private sale, and give a phone number where you can be reached. Then make sure you are around to answer the phone. Also, you should put an advertisement in your local paper. Your ad should be brief, but contain all the pertinent information a potential buyer would need: where the house is, how big it is (number of bedrooms), whether it has a garage and/or a basement, any special features (new wiring, plumbing, and so on), the price, and other details. This will help screen out unsuitable buyers. The ad should, therefore, be honest. You are just wasting your time, and your money, if you try to portray your two-room bungalow as a Georgian mansion in a Rhineland setting.

Your next step, once you've attracted your buyers, is to show them over your house. It's best to do this by appointment. For one thing, you'll be able to set the time of the appointment so that you can show your house to its best advantage. If your neighbor's dog howls like a werewolf from 9 a.m. to 5 p.m., then show your house in the evening. But if your neighbors have a habit of sitting on their porch in the evening drinking beer and lobbing their empties over the fence, then make sure you show the house during the day.

Once you have a would-be buyer inside your house, you should try to find out as much as you can (within reason) about him. Remember, you are now the salesman, and the art of selling lies in finding out what the buyer wants, and then giving it to him. That means emphasizing the strong features of your house — but only those that are likely to appeal to this particular would-be buyer. For example, if the buyer has two young children, the location of a school just up the road would be a feature to stress. But if the buyer has no children, then the close location of a school could be a drawback: The buyer might see it simply as a source of unwanted noise. Even so, you should point out such universal benefits as access to public transit, close proximity to shops, and other advantages of the neighborhood that the buyer might not be aware of. You're not just selling the house; you're also selling its location.

Perhaps the best rule to follow is: Be honest, and be silent. Don't misrepresent the house and its features in any way — that's self-defeating in the long run. At the same time, though, you don't have to offer negative information. If the buyer can't see that the house only has three walls, you're not obliged to point that out. If you want to be really efficient, you should prepare a list of all the relevant information a would-be buyer would need — price of the house, layout, size of rooms, mortgages, taxes, features, nearby facilities — so that the buyer can take it away with him. Also, you should be able to show receipts for any work you claim has been done on the house — a new roof, new plumbing — and show your monthly heating, hydro and tax bills to give the buyer an idea of the operating costs of your home.

Finally, when you find a buyer who is really serious, it's time to get something down on paper. Have the buyer complete an offer-to-purchase form (these are available from many stationery stores). And write in all the details of what exactly is being sold — the house and the land, obviously, but also the carpets, appliances, light shades, and so on, if they are to be included.

Arranging the financing is the buyer's responsibility, but you can help him (and thereby yourself) by being flexible. If the buyer doesn't have as much cash as you would like, for example, you could "take back" a second mortgage — but only if the sum of the mortgages is less than 75%-80% of the value of the house, and if the house is insured to the sum of the mortgages. You can always sell the second mortgage at a later date, but at a discount. At this late stage, though, you should be relying heavily on your lawyer. She will take care of most of the details for you, and see that you don't make any serious mistakes. Consult her whenever you like, no matter how small the point in contention. And never sign anything without first getting her advice.

Becoming a Landlord: it's easier than you think

Apartment vacancy rates have been edging lower in many Canadian cities, and as they continue to drop, the idea of investing in multi-unit buildings is becoming more appealing. Triplexes, four-plexes, ten-plexes and similar small multiples are especially appealing if you are looking for long-term gains and if you are willing to put in the extra effort and personal attention that this type of investment requires. To join the game, you usually need a 25% downpayment — say, $30,000-$50,000. Many families already have that kind of money in liquid investments such as savings accounts, bonds and stocks. Even if you haven't, don't count yourself out. If you're a homeowner, you may have discharged a mortgage. Or you may have paid it down substantially, thus building your equity. And your home itself has probably increased in value. By mortgaging or re-mortgaging, you may be able to get the funds for a new real estate investment.

As with any investment, though, before you do anything, you should realistically assess your goals. Are you out to make a big return or just to supplement your income? Or is your main aim capital gain? Then ask yourself how much you are prepared to risk. If it's a high-risk investment — and some experts insist that all real estate investments are high risk — are you prepared to lose your investment? Finally, how much effort are you prepared to put into your investment? If you're looking for a passive "sure thing," and you think rental collection is the essence of property management, forget it.

Unless you're buying at least 50 suites, you'll likely be your own property manager — and handyman, painter, plumber, electrician and janitor. Certainly, you can't be an absentee buyer of a four-plex and expect to make a profit. While the necessity for a hands-on approach deters some investors, it can actually be a source of profit. The handier you are with home maintenance and repairs, the more money you can save on operating expenses. Indeed, under rent controls, this can give you a critical advantage over other investors. Under Ontario's rent controls, for instance, you're free to boost rents by up to 6% per year. Anything over that requires application on a unit-by-unit basis to the Rent Review Board.

Just how much can you expect to make on a small multiple? And how much should you pay to buy one? Unfortunately, there's no single answer. You have to look over each individual deal. But given the right price and right location, you should experience good appreciation. Aside from short-term speculators and rooming-house operators, investors in small multiples have three investment goals:

* Long-term appreciation;
* Preservation of capital;
* Tax savings.

Long-term appreciation is probably the main goal, and the most realistic one among investors in small multiples. Rising construction costs alone mean that future units will cost more to duplicate. In addition, well-located rental apartment buildings may be torn down to make way for larger buildings. Apartments can be converted into offices or trendy boutiques and restaurants. Or they can be razed for luxury condominium or commercial structures.

Today, most investors put money into small multiples for capital appreciation rather than cash-on-cash. Cash-on-cash is a measure of return. It simply means the money you get back each year on your initial investment after paying mortgages and expenses, but before taxes. But to evaluate fully your return you should also look at equity build-up or amortization. This is the amount you pay off on your mortgage financing over the term of your investment. It doesn't mean cash in hand each month, but you realize it when you sell or refinance the property.

In inflationary times, investors also see small multiples as a way to preserve capital. And, unlike paper investments, property has the glitter of being tangible and subject to your direction.

Tax effects are also important. One big incentive to holding small multiples for appreciation is that capital gains are taxed, in effect, at half the rate of ordinary earned income. Furthermore, your taxable rental income is reduced by maintenance costs and depreciation. Since depreciation is a non-cash expense, you may end up with cash in hand. You'll eventually be taxed on any recaptured depreciation. But, in the meantime, you will have had the use of that deferred tax.

Your first task, though, will be figuring out just how much to pay for your small multiple. As with projected returns, there are no simple answers, no formulas that can be universally used. Indeed, the traditional techniques appraisers use for estimating value don't apply.

The best thing to do is look at comparable buildings in the market and then make sure the proposed rents are obtainable and that they'll be high enough to cover operating costs. For one thing, the more net income there is after covering costs, the more receptive a lender will be in helping you buy. Although you can probably find a lender for almost any building, provided you pay a high enough interest rate, most lenders prefer quality buildings with self-contained suites. However, some smaller trust companies and private sources will finance rooming houses or flats. Just because a lender advances you the money, though, don't think you've got a sound deal. Too often, the lender counts on the broker or buyer, and he, in turn, counts on the lender. For quality apartments, you can expect to pay the same rates as for a single family home, or at the most, ¼% more. A 25% down payment is usual. High-ratio insured loans can mean a better return. But be prepared, if the income doesn't materialize, to subsidize your mortgage payments from other sources.

Besides doing a financial analysis on any potential purchase, you should be looking at:

* Physical condition and functional qualities of the structure. These are the same things you would consider in buying your own home: everything from the condition of the roof to the adequacy of storage space. And, you should use professional inspection services if there's any doubt as to the condition, or if you're contemplating extensive renovations.
* Marketability. What is the demand for rental housing in your area? And what's the existing supply like? How much is there? What are the rents? Also, what neighborhood is the property in? Is there transportation? Shopping? Employment?

Each property must be individually analyzed in light of your own goals, the risks you're prepared to assume and the effort you're able to put into it. There are few certainties, so the risks will be fairly high. But then, too, so are the potential returns.

Real Estate Investment Trusts: liquid and stable

If you have been thinking of investing in the real estate market, but have been put off by the large amounts of capital that are sometimes required, then perhaps it is time to have another look. There are a number of sound real estate investments available, which offer a good return, but which do not demand the kind of initial outlay that might be beyond your reach. What we are talking about here, in other words, are the inexpensive real estate investments. You may be able to find other real estate ventures that promise a high return, low risk and favorable tax consequences. The investments we have selected offer these advantages, too, but bear in mind that they have been primarily chosen for their easy accessibility: You don't need much money to get involved.

At the top of any list of low-cost real estate investments would have to be paying off your own mortgage. Over the lifetime of most recent mortgages, you will be paying back about 2½-3 times the initial loan because of the high interest charges you will incur. If you can pay your mortgage principal off more quickly than your amortization table indicates, you will be able to reduce those interest payments and so, save yourself a considerable sum of money. Consequently, it is almost always worth your while to pay off your mortgage as quickly as your contract allows. If your present contract is particularly restrictive, and you foresee yourself being able to make a number of substantial prepayments, you might consider switching to one of the new types of mortgages. The only disadvantage to paying off your mortgage is that your investment is not very liquid: To turn it back into cash, you have to arrange a new mortgage or else sell your house.

Another inexpensive way in which you can participate in the real estate market is to put some of your money into a Real Estate Investment Trust (REIT). The return you get won't be as high as it would be if you were to pay off your mortgage, nor will the safety be as great (although it is still high). However, the return will usually be better than savings account interest, and the liquidity will be good. Essentially, a REIT invests in, and manages, a wide range of real estate mortgages and properties. It raises its capital for these investments through various debt instruments and by selling "units" to the investing public. This is how you can participate: by buying some of the units.

In essence, what you are buying are units similar to those offered by a mutual fund — except that in this case your money is being invested in mortgages or properties, and not in stocks. Under the rules establishing REITs— they were first set up in Canada in 1972 — a REIT is not required to pay income tax as long as it pays out at least 90% of its operating earnings in the form of dividends to unit holders. As a result, dividends are generally high. However, don't be lured only by the high dividends: Even if the REIT doesn't pay taxes, you do. And the dividends you receive will *not* qualify for the federal dividend tax credit. This is an important point to consider when assessing their relative merit. Dividend income from a REIT does, however, qualify for the $1,000 tax-free allowance of interest and dividend income.

It is possible that you have been put off the idea of investing in REITs because you have heard they have a poor reputation. This poor reputation, for weak management and subsequent bankruptcies, applied only to the U.S. REITs (where, incidentally, it was quite justified). In contrast, the Canadian REITs have been conservative and well managed, and their performance cannot really be compared with that of their U.S. counterparts. All five of the REITs are traded on the stock exchanges, so you can buy their units through your stockbroker. Generally, their prices tend to move slowly within a small range, because most people buy them for the dividends they pay. Don't buy them expecting large capital gains — you will be disappointed.

The big four REITs are: BBC Realty Investors, BM-RT Realty Investments, TD Realty Investments, and Canadian Realty Investors. The fifth and smallest REIT, GHI Mortgage Investors, specializes in riskier interim financing. Even so, it, too, has a record of steady growth under conservative management. Because they're traded on the stock exchanges, REIT units can be quickly converted into cash. The only possible exception to this would be GHI Mortgage Investors, because of its small float. Unit costs are relatively low too. Naturally, since you would be buying the REIT units through your broker, you would have to pay commissions, so you should aim for a minimum investment of 100 units; otherwise your brokerage commissions will be disproportionately high.

A third way to participate at low cost in the real estate market is to buy units in a trust company mortgage fund or in a mortgage and bond fund. These funds offer much the same advantages as REITs: good yield, safety, liquidity and stability. In this case, the funds take your money and invest it in mortgages and, if applicable, in high-quality corporate or government bonds. Like the REITs, the funds pay no income taxes, but again you, as a unit holder, would be taxed. (There would, of course, be no dividend tax credit here, because the income you would receive would be interest, not dividend.)

You can buy fund units from at least 16 trust companies and *caisses populaires.* For long-term performance comparisons of the different funds, you can check the financial papers or simply ask the funds themselves for their records of annual yields. Buying or selling the fund units doesn't involve any fees or commissions. However, there may be special charges for early redemption; and you generally have to give at least 30 days' notice before getting your money out. Minimum initial purchases are usually required to be $500. The funds redeem your units based on your proportionate share of the latest value placed on their investment portfolio. This means the value of your units will change. But, as in the case of REITs, the variations, particularly for the larger funds, are usually only a few percentage points either way. So, again, don't expect significant capital gains.

Another popular way to invest in real estate is to buy and sell the shares of publicly listed companies. Several have shown steady and high compound rates of return for the past seven years. And there is still the possibility of takeovers or buy-backs of one or two smaller companies. These could benefit minority shareholders to the extent that the buy-back or takeover bid exceeds the prevailing market price.